Paris for Foodies:

The Ultimate Guide to Eating in Paris

Frédéric BIBARD (TalkinFrench.com)

"Best blog dedicated to the French Language and Culture for 2014."

(Voted by the Language Portal bab.la and its community)

Contents

Introduction

Welcome to Paris! Now let's explore the exquisite French cuisine.

Hello, traveler! Bonjour! Part of the fun of traveling is sampling local food. This is especially necessary when visiting a place like Paris. There is simply no other way to do it: food belongs at the top of every Parisian travel checklist. France is, after all, the gastronomic capital of the world, and apart from seeing the famous sights, what trip would be complete without getting a taste of authentic French cuisine in the country's capital?

Paris is dotted with endless dining options. From quaint cafes, picture-perfect bistros, tempting patisseries, and fancy Michelin-starred restaurants to tiny home-style kitchens, rustic brasseries, and ultra-chic modern gastropubs, the options are endless. The plethora of fine dining restaurants run by big-name celebrity chefs contrast with well-concealed joints which are little more than homey kitchens serving a handful of guests, but both provide the most exquisitely authentic French fare you will ever try.

Time and budget, however, play a crucial part in determining which cafes to visit, which restaurant to have dinner in, or which bistro food to sample. Even though spontaneity is a fun trait to have when going on an adventure, it is quite advisable to have a bit of insider background to point you in the right direction.

...And meet this book, too.

Finding the right restaurant can be such a hassle, especially one with the right mix of quality, value, and location. And, of course, most travelers do not have the luxury of time to spend gallivanting around in search for the right restaurant.

That is where this book comes in. This book gives you:

- **The 10 best places to dine per arrondissement.** To make things easier for you, this helpful book will give you ten good options you can pick from when you find yourself in a certain Parisian district. The best spots to enjoy a meal are all grouped into the 20 different arrondissements or districts they are located in, so you do not have to shuffle around aimlessly or jump from place to place all in search of a good place to eat.
- **A price range to suit your budget.** Whether the sky's the limit for your wallet or you are looking to fit everything in a shoestring budget, this book gives you the price range for each restaurant. This can be especially handy for the budget-conscious ones who do not want to sacrifice value either.
- **Opening Hours.** The worst thing is to head over to a special restaurant only to discover that it is not open during your visit. Awful, right? There is, however a way to avoid this: simply check out the opening hours in this book to make sure you are visiting at a good time.
- **The nearest subway station.** No need to scour the internet for directions -- the nearest station is conveniently listed to help you easily find your way to the location.
- **The exact address.** This one is added as well to guide you to the exact location.
- **Insider tidbits.** The book also covers interesting tidbits about the places listed, as well as some good tips and helpful bits of information, including great conversation starters.

And ...

- **EVEN MORE LISTS!** Aside from the top ten dining options per district, you will also see several other lists covering dining options for different needs, such as gluten-free and vegetarian restaurants for those with dietary restrictions, restaurants perfect for families, must-try street foods, must-order French dishes, dining spots that serve meals for less than 10 euros, and more thoughtful information you will need to thoroughly enjoy your trip.

In short, this book has everything you need to know about where you can pick up the best eats at the nearest places to where your activities are.

Keep in mind, however, that the top ten lists per arrondissement are listed in no particular order. They are the best ones you can find in an area, catering to a wide range of budgets and tastes, and they are guaranteed to give you an out-of-this-world gastronomic experience.

First, Some Background.

French chefs are widely known all over the world for creating amazingly mouth-watering and elegant gourmet food. Infusing creativity with traditional French cooking techniques and practices, French cuisine has set a standard of excellence and contributed to culinary education; it was even added to UNESCO's list of the world's intangible cultural heritage. For this reason, French people are highly appreciative of fine food, even at a young age, and take pride in the wonderful reputation of amazing French cuisine.

What is known today as classic French cuisine dates back to as early as the 17th century, when two chefs paved the way for the distinct French style of cooking to emerge. Before this, French cuisine was largely influenced by the Italians, and it was only when chefs François Pierre La Varenne and Marie-Antoine Carême decided to shift from foreign influences that French gastronomy began to take shape.

By the 20th century, French ways of cooking became standardized and codified into what later became the high-level, elite gastronomic experience known as *haute cuisine*. In the '70s, the nouvelle cuisine (new cuisine) became popular and was focused on fewer ingredients and more flexible methods.

Today, we can experience a French cuisine which is characterized by creative experimentation on non-traditional flavors while preserving its usual wonderful presentation and spectacular taste – one that has influenced and won the world over.

What Makes it Different?

As many of us know, French food is unique. But what *really* makes it different?
Three things in particular make French cuisine stand out: the ingredients, the presentation, and the approach as an art form.

The ingredients. The lovely climate in France makes it possible for high-quality ingredients to be produced. French cooks take advantage of this and make sure everything is freshly picked and cooked to perfection, from herbs, which are featured heavily in French cooking, to local produce. Here are the ingredients you will find most common in French dishes:

- Meats are often the star of the show in French meals. Beef, pork, poultry, game meats, and charcuterie (ham, sausage and cold cuts) are all top favorites.
- Vegetables – the freshest and the ripest – are carefully picked and prepared. These are then cooked into side dishes or as part of the main course. Favorite veggies include leafy greens, tomatoes, onions, eggplant, carrots, and zucchini. Truffles and other locally grown fungi and mushrooms are also commonly used.
- Cheeses! The French people's love affair with cheese is quite evident every which way in Paris. France is home to about 500 different types of cheese, with each region producing their own kinds of cheese. French cuisine pays tribute to this every so often.

The presentation. French food is quite aesthetically pleasing. Extra care is taken to ensure the food looks beautiful on the plate, making it not only pleasing to the taste buds, but to the eyes as well. So bust out your cameras and get ready! Each plate is truly Instagram-worthy!

The art form. French cooking involves a wide variety of techniques. They can be extremely complicated and therefore require careful preparation and an ample amount of time to accomplish. To master this level of art form, you need a certain amount of precision, practice, and creativity. Years of meticulous practice and study have transformed French cuisine into an art form, which is why mastering it is considered by many to be the highest level of culinary success.

Make sure to keep an eye out for these elements when you dine out in Paris. It will help you appreciate the thorough selection, utmost care, and level of passion and creativity that goes into each and every plate.

A Few Basics Before We Proceed.

Here is a list of terms you will need to get acquainted with before you proceed with this book and onward to your great French food adventure.

The French meals:

·   **Le petit déjeuner** (breakfast) – usually simple and consists of bread or a pastry and a hot drink (coffee, tea, or hot chocolate).

·   **Le déjeuner** (lunch) – lunch is a leisurely affair traditionally consisting of several courses. But traditions are shifting and you can now just as easily set up a lovely picnic outdoors with some cheeses and a baguette.

·   **Le dîner** (dinner) – dinner for the French is a more elaborate affair. It is a special time for loved ones to gather and talk about the day and enjoy each other's company over good food and beverages. It consists of several courses, starting with appetizers and ending with dessert;

a cheese course (fromage) may be included after the main course. Bread and wine are also present during most dinners.

The drinks:

French people like to have a round of drinks before and after a meal. The drinks before a meal are called *apéritifs* (which literally means *appetite opener*) while the drinks after a meal are called *digestifs* (stronger alcohol which supposedly helps with digestion).

· **Happy hour!** – The French have adopted this custom, and some bistros and cafes offer good prices for their best cocktails and wines between 6 and 8 in the evening -- just in time for some "apéritif!"

· **Alcoholic drinks** – You can find more alcoholic beverages at supermarkets, wine shops, or grocers. Just remember that, in dining establishments, wine or beer with less than 15 degrees in alcohol strength may be served to under-18 guests, but spirits are not allowed.

The legal drinking age in France is 16 years old for wine and beer and 18 years old for spirits and liquor. No matter what age you are, however, keep in mind that French culture -- as well as the rest of polite society -- frowns upon excessive drinking and rowdy, drunk behavior.

The different kinds of food establishments:

You will come across a wide variety of dining options in Paris. To help you sort through the pile and figure out which is which and what is what, here is a short primer for you.

Restaurant – Paris spawned the idea of the modern restaurant, and even the name itself was coined in 18ᵗʰ century Paris. To date, there are more than 5,000 restaurants in Paris alone.

Bistro – a smaller, cozier version of a restaurant that often features chalkboard menus and regional dishes.

Bistrot à Vin – can be likened to vintage-style cabarets and tavernes, which offer alcoholic drinks and simple food.

Brasserie – serves beer, wine, coffee, and meals and are open all day, every day. Some versions feature an old-fashioned setup with a drugstore.

Café – the chic little place that offers limited kinds of food and often has outdoor seating.

Salon de Thé – this is just like the cafe. It serves tea, hot chocolate, coffee, and some snacks and salads.

Bar – influenced by the American bars, the French bars also serve all kinds of alcoholic beverages and, in some cases, a few simple dishes and sandwiches.

Auberge – a restaurant usually attached to a hotel.

Buvette – a small kiosk that sells food like sandwiches, ice creams, or drinks.

Cafétéria – offers basic meals and drinks.

Crêperie – serves crêpes with either sweet or savory fillings.

Estaminet – a small, often seedy bar.

Rôtisserie – also known as a Grill and usually serves a wide range of food but specializes in grilled and roasted dishes.

So, now that we have covered the basics, are you ready for a gastronomic adventure of astronomic proportions? Your book is ready to guide you there.

Have fun and *bonne chance*!

French Restaurant Etiquette:

Make dinner reservations for small or upscale restaurants in advance

Reserve a table, unless you are heading to McDonald's or a neighborhood café. If you are running late, call the restaurant or you may arrive to find someone else sitting at your table. If you cannot honor the reservation, call and cancel as early in the day as possible. It is polite, as most good French restaurants have a waiting list. Who knows, you may be on it next time.

Ordering

In France, diners do not always order their entire meal at once. Instead, the waiter will often go around taking appetizer orders first, then return for the main course orders. Only after all food orders have been taken will drinks be ordered.
Note: Aperitif orders will be taken upon arrival.

Changes to the menu

What you see is what you get. The French will not customize your dish by adding or removing ingredients, nor will they accept orders for items that are not on the menu. This could be the single most important difference between North American and French dining etiquette. The French chef has prepared the dish for you with love and has put a lot of thought into the end product. The flavors all make sense together. You cannot make any changes without truly vexing the chef, the server, and subsequently all of the locals with whom you are dining. In the U.S., the client is king, but in France, it is the chef who takes charge of the show. It may not be an easy point to grasp, but it is important to remember when dining in France.

What to do with your hands

For some reason, it is very rude to keep your hands in your lap while you are dining in France. It is equally rude to keep your elbows on the table. Therefore, the tourist diner must keep his or her hands, and not the elbows, visible. Also remember that the French almost never eat with their hands. This includes the so-called "finger foods."

The bread

Bread will always be served with your meal. If you are dining formally, bread will be served on its own plate. However, if you have no bread plate, the bread rests on the table cloth and not on your plate. There is also a certain manner in which you should eat bread. While most Americans may take a bite out of the bread, the French consider taking a bite out of a whole slice of bread to be rather boorish. Instead, tear off the bread piece by piece. If you are using bread to soak up sauce, spear it with a fork instead of holding it with your hand.

Follow the leader

The number one rule in French dining etiquette is to follow the host. If you do this and observe carefully, you will almost never err. This is particularly important as we are discussing first learning to eat or drink in France. In general, it is polite to wait until everyone has been served and then the host will begin eating. Likewise, if there is an aperitif served, you should wait until the host raises her glass before you raise yours and take a drink.

Eating Out

Following the tips above will save you from making too many embarrassing faux pas. While the rules of eating do not change drastically when you are eating out, there are a few special considerations to remember.

Service Compris

In America, the standard tip in a nice restaurant is between 15% and 20%. In France, tips are included in the price. This is a French law that ensures the tips can be assessed for taxation purposes. You will see a *service compris* on your bill which will be 15% of your food. However, one nice thing is that the price of food includes both the tip and the tax. So, for example, if you order a piece of cake for $5 and a cup of coffee for $3, your bill is $8 -- *service compris!*

Leaving and paying

This is not as easy as it might seem. As the concept of tipping is not a necessity, there is less pressure for quick table turnover. In France, you may enjoy your meal as long as you wish — your waiter will not want to hurry you out. When you are ready for the check, do not be shy. Ask. If you are not successful, stand, go to the front of the restaurant, and if you are really desperate, make as if you are leaving. Strangely, the check will appear!

How To Tip In Paris:

Cafés

When having drinks, although not necessary, people often leave the change. If the bill is €3.80, you can leave 4€. 5€ is excessive, unless you have accidentally smashed the table in half or something.
Simply round it off to the nearest whole. At the bar, if a coffee is €1.20, you can leave an extra 10-20 *centimes* behind if you want.

Meals and Restaurants

In most restaurants, including cafés, one can leave €1 for every €20. So, if the check is €80, you can leave anywhere from €2 - €4. Think of it as a kind gesture, not an obligation. Once again, it is not necessary but it is appreciated for good service.
In nicer restaurants, such as 3-star places where the service is exemplary, a tip of €20 is fine to leave. It is not necessary to tip the coat check person. When in doubt, look at French diners and see what they leave as a gratuity.

Coat Check

In simple restaurants, if the waiter grabs your coats and puts them on the hook, there is no need to tip. However, in a nicer restaurant, especially if there is a coat check, €1 per coat is expected.

10 Best Restaurants for 1st Arrondissement:

The 1st Arrondissement is located in the very heart of Paris. It is walking distance from most tourist sites and landmarks, such as the Louvre, the Tuileries, and the Palais-Royal. In the 1st, you can find some of the finest and most luxurious restaurants in Paris, but we included some awesome affordable restaurants in our list as well.

1. L'Absinthe

While still being a casual and comfortable bistro, L'Absinthe has been taken up a few notches since it is now owned by Caroline Rostang, the daughter of the French culinary chef Michel Rostang. It is described as being similar to the New York City vibe: trendy, charming, and chic, yet traditional at the same time.

Hours: Monday - Thursday for lunch (12:00 pm - 2:15 pm) and dinner (7:00 pm - 10:15 pm). Closes at 10:45 pm on Friday and Saturday.
Price Range: €11 - €45
Closest Subway Station: Opéra
Address: 24 Place du Marché Saint-Honoré, 75001 Paris

2. Yam'Tcha

A fusion of French and Asian cuisine, Yam'Tcha is a Michelin Star restaurant, so expect to spend some bucks. Owned by Adeline Grattard, who spent many years in Asia, the intimate dining room is decorated with tasteful Asian accents, has a calm atmosphere, and employs highly experienced chefs, making it a perfect place to eat. But do book in advance!
Hours: Wednesday - Sunday, 11:30 am - 7:30 pm. Closed Monday and Tuesday.
Price Range: €35 - €99
Closest Subway Station: Louvre-Rivoli or Les Halles
Address: 121 Rue Saint Honoré, 75001 Paris

3. Le Meurice

Considered one of the best restaurants in Paris, Le Meurice is a Michelin 3-starred restaurant. It is a destination for gastronomes from all over the world as they tour the richness of French flavors while enjoying royal and romantic settings. Surprisingly, it is also family-friendly, loaning children custom-made boats to sail in the pond in the nearby Tuileries.

Hours: Monday - Friday for lunch (12:30 pm - 2:30 pm) and dinner (7:30 pm - 10:00 pm). Open for breakfast from 7:00 am to 10:30 am during the weekdays and from 7:00 am to 11:30 am on weekends.
Price Range: €35 - €130
Closest Subway Station: Tuileries: line 1
Address: 228 Rue de Rivoli, 75001 Paris

4.   Le First

Have lunch with a stunning view of Tuileries Jardins at Le First restaurant Boudoir! Try to book a table by the window or the outdoor terrace. The interiors are also elegantly chic. Pair that with Michelin-level dishes and you have an amazing gastronomic experience.

Hours: Sunday - Saturday, 12:00 pm - 3:00 pm and 7:00 pm - 11:00 pm
Price Range: €21 - €52
Closest Subway Station: Tuileries
Address: 234 rue de Rivoli 75001 Paris

5. Chez Denise

This is the place to be if you like to have a good time with good company! By midnight, the place is brimming with a hungry and happy vibe. You can try traditional savory dishes and wash them down with the house Brouilly wine for a reasonable price. It is the perfect place to share dishes, too, as the portions are very generous.

Hours: Monday - Friday for lunch (12:00 pm to 3:00 pm) and for dinner (7:30 pm to 5:00 am). Closed Saturday and Sunday.
Price Range: €21 - €40
Closest Subway Station: Les Halles (4, RER A, B)
Address: 5 Rue des Prouvaires, 75001 Paris

6. L'Ardoise

One of the city's finest modern bistros, L'Ardoise a tiny storefront decorated with enlargements of old sepia postcards depicting Paris. The seating is tight and it is always crowded, so be sure to book in advance. This chef-owned establishment offers some superb cuisine at a reasonable price.

Hours: Tuesday - Saturday for lunch (12:00 pm - 2:30 pm) and for dinner (7:00 pm to 11:00 pm), and Sunday for dinner only (from 7:00 pm to 11:00 pm). Closed Monday.
Price Range: €21 - €40
Closest Subway Station: Tuileries
Address: 28 Rue du Mont Thabor, 75001 Paris

7.   Pirouette

Unlike many restaurants that only serve specific dishes daily, Pirouette strongly promotes clients' freedom of choice. Restaurant goers have the option of selecting one of five starters, one of five main courses, and one of five desserts that change every month. Stylish, relaxed, and with incredibly affordable prices, you will not be disappointed eating here.

Hours: Monday - Saturday for lunch (12:30 pm - 2:30 pm) and dinner (7:30 pm - 10:30 pm). Closed Sunday.
Price Range: €21 - €49
Closest Subway Station: Les Halles (1, 4, 7, 11); Etienne Marcel (4)
Address: 5 Rue Mondétour, 75001 Paris

8. Spring

Owned and operated by Chicago-born, French-trained chef Daniel Rose, it is probably one of the most recognized restaurants in Paris. If you are lucky enough, you will get to sit upstairs and watch the team of chefs create masterpieces thanks to Spring's open kitchen concept. Spring does not have a standard menu -- you are served the menu of the day based on what is fresh and in season when you visit.

Hours: Tuesday - Saturday for dinner (6:30 pm - 10:30 pm). Closed Sunday and Monday.
Price Range: €41 - €100
Closest Subway Station: Louvre-Rivoli (1)
Address: 6 Rue Bailleul, 75001 Paris

9. Ferdi

The motto of this small restaurant, as clearly stated on the front door, is, "Good food takes time," and rightfully so. The restaurant is named after the Fontanier's son Ferdinand and is, interestingly enough, decorated with his old toys and framed family photos. Ferdi is known for its delicious cheeseburgers, and I recommend you reserve a table if you want to try one for dinner.

Hours: Monday - Friday (6:30 pm - 11:30 pm), Saturday (1:30 pm - 11:30 pm) and Sunday (6:30 pm - 11:30 pm).
Price Range: €21 - €40
Closest Subway Station: Tuileries
Address: 32 Rue du Mont Thabor, 75001 Paris

10. Issé

One of the best Japanese restaurants in Paris, Izakaya Issé is original and highly inventive. It is known for having the best sake menu in Paris, and if you do not know much about sake, don't worry -- a server will be happy to help you learn! Issé is definitely a high fashion restaurant, so expect to spend some cash here.

Hours: Monday - Saturday for lunch (12:00 pm - 2:00 pm) and dinner (7:00 pm - 11:00 pm). Closed Sunday.
Price Range: €20 - €57
Closest Subway Station: Pyramides (7, 14)
Address: 45 Rue de Richelieu, 75001 Paris

10 Best Restaurants for 2nd Arrondissement:

The Second Arrondissement is in the heart of Paris and is close to many tourist attractions, fabulous shopping, and great restaurants. It is also one of the financial centers of Paris, home to the Bourse (Stock exchange). Great restaurants and small cafes are plentiful in this area.

1. Chez Georges

Dating back to 1926, there are not very many places left like Chez Georges in Paris. It is one of the best-preserved bistros in the city. Chez Georges offers the elegance and ambience of an authentic Parisian bistro while serving the classics of French cuisine.

Hours: Monday - Friday for lunch (12:30 pm - 2:30 pm) and dinner (7:00 pm - 11:00 pm). Closed Saturday and Sunday.
Price Range: €29 - €100
Closest Subway Station: Bourse (3)
Address: 1 Rue du Mail, 75002 Paris

2. Drouant

With elegant, richly decorated interiors and facing a pretty square, Drouant has been around even longer than Chez Georges. Now run by Antoine Westermann, the menu offers traditional cuisine with a modern touch.

Hours: Monday to Sunday (12:00 pm - 12:00 am).
Price Range: €21 - €100
Closest Subway Station: 4 Septembre (3)
Address: 16 Rue Gaillon, 75002 Paris

3. Fontaine Gaillon

If you are a wine lover, this is the place for you! The vinotheque is set in the middle of the dining room, boasting over 150 wines selections. Located near the Opera Garnier, it is the perfect place for pre-opera dinners or business lunches. Fontaine Gaillon is known for serving quality food at affordable prices.

Hours: Monday - Friday for lunch (12:00 pm - 2:30 pm) and dinner (7:00 pm - 11:30 pm). Closed Saturday and Sunday.
Price Range: €21 - €110
Closest Subway Station: Quatre Septembre (M3)
Address: 1 Rue de la Michodière, 75002 Paris

4. Bistro Volnay

Owned by two young women, Bistro Volany is an Art-Deco inspired restaurant with a beautiful 1930's bar, big mirrors in the dining room, and glowing lamps. If you are young or young at heart, this is the place to be, as many young hip Parisians tend to frequent this bistro. Its menu is a perfect balance of tradition and modern twists.

Hours: Monday - Friday for lunch (12:00 pm - 2:30 pm) and dinner (7:00 pm - 10:00 pm). Closed Saturday and Sunday.
Price Range: €8 - €49
Closest Subway Station: Opéra (3, 7, 8)
Address: 8 Rue Volney, 75002 Paris

5. Frenchie

Today, eating at a restaurant in an alley is utterly cool and hip, especially with the name Frenchie! The chef, who earned the nickname Frenchie at Jamie Oliver's in London, has a frequently changing menu that features fresh greens and amazing flavors. Since it is a small and very popular spot, you have to book weeks, if not months, in advance. Another alternative if you do not get to score a table in the dining room is the wine bar across the street, also owned by Frenchie. It serves similar food in a more casual atmosphere.

Hours: Monday - Friday (6:30 pm - 10:00 pm). Closed Saturday and Sunday.
Price Range: €21 - €100
Closest Subway Station: Sentier (3)
Address: 5 Rue du Nil, 75002 Paris

6. Aux Lyonnais

Dedicated to preserving culinary traditions of Lyon, Aux Lyonnais is housed in a historic 1890's building. This restaurant's specialty is serving its guests updated versions of traditional Lyonnais dishes, such as frog legs and farm-raised chicken casserole. Come here with an adventurous palate and you will not go home disappointed.

Hours: Tuesday - Friday for lunch (12:00 pm - 2:00 pm) and dinner (7:30 pm - 10:00 pm). Saturday for dinner only (7:30 pm - 10:00 pm). Closed Sunday and Monday.
Price Range: €21 - €49
Closest Subway Station: Richelieu Drouot (8, 9) or Bourse (3)
Address: 32 Rue Saint-Marc, 75002 Paris

7. Le Petit Vendôme

You will always find a long line stretching out of the door of Le Petit Vendôme during peak hours. Why, you ask? Well, because they are waiting to eat some of the best sandwiches in Paris served on some amazingly tasty baguettes from Boulangerie Julien (the best baguettes in Paris). I recommend you go for lunch and take your delicious sandwich to the Tuileries gardens to eat while gazing out on the Louvre. If sandwiches are not your thing, you can opt to sit down at a table and have a hearty meal at an affordable price! Keep in mind that sandwiches are not served at the tables (sandwiches are considered as a take away food).

Hours: Monday (8:00 am - 6:00 pm), Tuesday - Friday (8:00 am - 11:30 pm), and Saturday (8:00 am - 6:30 pm). Closed Sunday.
Price Range: €8 - €20
Closest Subway Station: Opéra (3, 7, 8)
Address: 8 Rue des Capucines, 75002 Paris

8. L'Ecaille de la Fontaine

This great seafood restaurant is owned by actor Gerard Depardieu. Known for offering some of the best oyster platters, shellfish, and seafood in the city, L'Ecaille de la Fontaine was designed to be a less expensive option to the Fontaine Gaillon across the street. If you want good, fresh, superb seafood in a cozy setting, then this is your spot!

Hours: Monday - Friday for lunch (12:00 pm - 2:30 pm) and dinner (7:00 pm - 11:30 pm). Closed Saturday and Sunday.
Price Range: €40 - €50
Closest Subway Station: Quatre-Septembre
Address: 15 Rue Gaillon, 75002 Paris

9. Le Versance

This restaurant is a stylish fine-dining destination, decorated with plush gray chairs, ironed white tablecloths, stained glass windows, and rustic wooden ceiling beams. Once home to Le Petit Coin de la Bourse, it has been reinvented by the chef Samuel Cavagnis. It is a great spot to go with your significant other because of its elegance, decent seating space for enjoying a private conversation, and refined and creative dishes.

Hours: Tuesday - Friday for lunch (12:00 pm - 2:00 pm) and dinner (8:00 pm - 10:00 pm). Saturday for dinner only (8:00 pm - 10:00 pm). Closed Sunday and Monday.
Price Range: €41 and above
Closest Subway Station: Bourse
Address: 16 Rue Feydeau, 75002 Paris

10. Passage 53

Although the decor is minimalist, the food is anything but. Japanese chef Shinichi Sato's Asian-inspired contemporary French cuisine is so carefully crafted it looks like an art piece on a plate. Using market fresh produce, this restaurant has already earned its second Michelin star.

Hours: Closed Sunday and Monday. Open Tuesday - Saturday for lunch (12:00 pm - 2:30 pm) and dinner (8:00 pm - 9:30 pm).
Price Range: €35 - €100
Closest Subway Station: Grands Boulevards (8,9)
Address: 53 Passage des Panoramas, 75002 Paris

10 Best Restaurants for 3rd Arrondissement:

The 3rd Arrondissement is in the upper Marais district near the beautiful Place de Vosges. It is a busy and vibrant location. There are several good open air markets, a gigantic covered flea market, and lots of great specialty food stores, as well a host of fantastic restaurants.

1.   Au Bascou

The chef at Au Bascou is from the Basque region of France (southwest), so expect to see and taste some Basque influences on your plate. This is a great place to get a 'local' feel, as most of the restaurant visitors are locals. A modern bistro with quirky decor including ochre-hued walls, oil paintings, and objects of the southwestern region of France, the smells and aromas coming from the kitchen are so alluring you might be tempted to order everything on the menu!

Hours: Monday - Friday for lunch (12:00 pm - 2:00 pm) and dinner (7:30 pm - 10:30 pm). Closed Saturday and Sunday.
Price Range: €21 - €40
Closest Subway Station: Arts et Métiers
Address: 38 Rue Réaumur, 75003 Paris

2.   Ambassade d'Auvergne

A charming and inviting place for simple and rustic but incredibly delicious food! The name describes this restaurant to a tee -- they truly are ambassadors of the Auvergne region of France. The dishes are all Auvergne specialties, like the rôti d'agneau, which arrives as a pot of melting chunks of lamb in a rich, meaty sauce with a helping of tender white beans (yum!). Even the regional wines are served here: Chanturgue, Boudes, and Madargues.

Hours: Monday - Sunday for lunch (12:00 pm - 2:00 pm) and dinner (7:30 pm - 10:00 pm).
Price Range: €8 - €33
Closest Subway Station: Rambuteau
Address: 22 Rue du Grenier Saint-Lazare, 75003 Paris

3.   Le 404

Travel to Morocco in France simply by visiting Le 404! Located in an old 16th-century building, this magnificent restaurant is known for its lively atmosphere, incomparable Moroccan and Berber specialties, and affordable prices. Its weekend brunch is very popular, so reservations are advised. If you have been in Paris for a while and want to try something other than French cuisine, this is totally the place for you.

Hours: Monday - Sunday for lunch (12:30 pm - 2:00 pm) and dinner (8:00 pm - 12:00 am).
Price Range: €8 - €40
Closest Subway Station: Métro Arts & Métiers
Address: 69 Rue des Gravilliers, 75003 Paris

4. Le Petit Dakar

Again, if you want to try some amazing food but also want to experience variety, try Le Petit Dakar. As the name suggests, Le Petit Dakar specializes in Senegalese cuisine, yet not all of the dishes on the menu are from Senegal. The entire series of entrées is listed under the title "Un Détour par les Iles" (An Island Detour), which acknowledges the culinary culture of France's departmental and territorial island. Cool! Inside, works of colorful, contemporary, multi-media African art decorate the walls while African music plays in the background.

Hours: Tuesday - Saturday for lunch (12:30 pm - 2:30 pm) and dinner (7:30 pm - 10:30 pm). Sunday for dinner only (7:30 pm - 10:30 pm). Closed Monday.
Price Range: €15 - €22
Closest Subway Station: Saint-Paul | Plan d'accès
Address: 6 Rue Elzevir, 75003 Paris

5. Breizh Café

If you are craving some exceptional, wildly raved-about crepes and galettes, this is a good place to go. It is best to make reservations, though, as this place can get packed with both locals and tourists.

Hours: Sunday (11:30 am - 10:00 pm), and Wednesday - Saturday (11:30 am - 11:00 pm). Closed Monday and Tuesday.
Price Range: €11 - €20
Closest Subway Station: Saint-Sébastien - Froissart
Address: 109 rue Vieille du Temple, 75003 Paris

6. L'estaminet d'Arômes & Cépages

L'estaminet (meaning "small public house") is a lively little cafe and wine bar located inside Paris' oldest covered market, the Marché des Enfants-Rouge. A welcoming wooden country door marks the entrance, and inside you will find communal tables and charming decor that create a relaxing country atmosphere. The menu is made up of mostly organic ingredients. Plates of cheese and charcuterie, tartines, salads, and soups are just examples of what this great-tasting place has to offer. There are also organic wines available.

Hours: Tuesday - Saturday (9:00 am - 8:00 pm), and Sunday (9:00 am - 3:00 pm). Closed Monday.
Price Range: €20 - €30
Closest Subway Station: Arts-et-Metiers, Filles du Calvaire
Address: 39 rue de Bretagne, 75003 Paris, France

7. Auberge Nicolas Flamel

Located in a 1407 building which happens to be the oldest stone house in Paris, Auberge Nicolas Flamel is a fine dining restaurant named after the renowned alchemist and owner of the house. Apart from the wonderful history of the place, the restaurant is widely known for its exquisite dishes and reasonable prices for the quality of food and service it provides.

Hours: Monday - Saturday for lunch (12:00 pm - 2:30 pm) and dinner (7:00 pm - 10:30 pm)
Price Range: €18 - €55
Closest Subway Station: Rambuteau
Address: 51 rue Montmorency, 75003 Paris

8. Pramil

Good food and good value. This is a small, intimate restaurant that will surprise you with its creative and flavorful dishes.

Hours: Monday - Saturday (12:00 pm - 2:30 pm), Monday only (7:30 pm - 10:30 pm), and Tuesday - Sunday (7:00 pm - 10:30 pm).
Price Range: €33 - €48
Closest Subway Station: Temple
Address: 9 rue Vertbois 75003 Paris

9. Chez Janou

The crowd at Chez Janou is mixed, attractive, and lively, making it hard not to be in a good mood here. It is the perfect mix between typical Provencal bistro and crowded Parisian bistro atmosphere. If it is nice out, the terrace is amazing, especially on Sundays. It also has more than 80 varieties of pastis you can try!

Hours: Monday - Sunday for lunch (12:00 pm - 3:00 pm) and dinner (7:00 pm - 10:30 pm).
Price Range: €8 - €20
Closest Subway Station: Chemin Vert
Address: 2 Rue Roger Verlomme, 75003 Paris

10. Café Pinson

For some homemade organic options with a cozy and artsy ambiance, Café Pinson is the way to go. With great food that caters to people with dietary restrictions, and while still managing to make it taste amazing, this place is indeed a standout.

Hours: Sunday (10:00 am - 6:00 pm), Monday - Friday (9:00 am - 12:00 am), and Saturday (10:00 am - 12:00 am).
Price Range: €11 - €20
Closest subway station: Filles du Calvaire
Address: 6 rue du Forez 75003 Paris

10 Best Restaurants for 4th Arrondissement:

The 4th Arrondissement lies along the Seine and on the Ile St. Louis. The 4th is a good chunk of what used to be medieval Paris and is near Notre Dame and the Hotel du Ville. It is a lush area also known for its beautiful bridges.

1. Le Georges

Le Georges is a favorite spot among many, and for an obvious reason: it is located on top of the Centre Georges Pompidou (home of the Musée National d'Art Moderne), which gives its guests a breathtaking panoramic view of the city. The restaurant has an interesting minimalist interior which makes you feel like you have jumped into The Space Odyssey movie, and the menu features a trendy fusion-cuisine. Although the fare is a bit above average, you cannot complain when you are wining and dining while enjoying an amazing view of Paris. Be sure to make a reservation and request a table outside!

Hours: Monday for lunch and dinner (12:00 pm - 1:00 am), Wednesday - Sunday for lunch and dinner (12:00 pm to 1:00 am). Closed Tuesday.
Price Range: €21 - €40
Closest Subway Station: M° Rambuteau, M° Hôtel de Ville
Address: 6ème étage, Le Centre Pompidou, Palais Beaubourg, Place Georges Pompidou, 75004 Paris

2. L' Ambroisie

Super fancy, classy, sophisticated, and pricey, this is a place to visit for special occasions. This 3-starred Michelin restaurant is located on the beautiful Place de Vosges. With an intimate interior that evokes 17th-century France, L'Ambroisie serves the best French haute cuisine. It is also known for its excellent service -- the staff pampers and spoils their guests. You get what you pay for, right?

Hours: Tuesday - Saturday for lunch (12:00 pm - 2:00 pm) and dinner (7:00 pm - 10:30 pm). Closed Sunday and Monday.
Price Range: €210 - €330
Closest Subway Station: Saint-Paul (1)
Address: 9 Place des Vosges, 75004 Paris

3. Bofinger

Founded in 1864, Brasserie Bofinger is considered to be the most beautiful brasserie in Paris. Serving a mix of traditional French recipes and Alsatian specialties, it is best known for its Sauerkrauts and seafood. It is beautifully decorated with moleskin banquettes, paintings by Hansi on the first floor, and a ground-floor glass canopy which creates a unique and cheerful atmosphere.

Hours: Monday - Friday for lunch (12:00 pm - 3:00 pm) and dinner (6:30 pm - 1:00 am), Saturday and Sunday (12:00 pm - 1:00 am).
Price Range: €21 - €40
Closest Subway Station: Bastille

Address: 5-7 Rue de la Bastille, 75004 Paris

4. Le Trumilou

A favorite among locals, Le Trumilou is a family owned restaurant. Serving traditional French home-cooking, this bistro makes you feel like you are eating at someone's grandmother's house. Super traditional and authentic with very fair prices, you will not be disappointed with Le Trumilou.

Hours: Monday - Sunday for lunch (12:00 pm - 3:00 pm) and dinner (7:30 pm - 11:00 pm).
Price Range: €8 - €20
Closest Subway Station: Pont Marie
Address: 84 Quai de l'Hôtel de ville, 75004 Paris

5. Au Bougnat

Known for authentic and refined cuisine served in a traditional, simple, and warm setting, Au Bougnat offers a seasonal menu, giving its guests delicious, fresh ingredients. This bistro has affordable menu items and fixed-price options, something that is particularly appreciated in this touristy part of town.

Hours: Monday - Sunday for lunch and dinner (12:00 pm - 10:00 pm).
Price Range: €21 - €40
Closest Subway Station: Cité
Address: 26 Rue Chanoinesse, 75004 Paris

6. Chez Julien

One of Marais's hippest spots, Chez Julien welcomes you into their retro space and offers you classic French dishes. In the winter, sit inside and enjoy the cozy, intimate atmosphere while being surrounded by 1900-style decor. In the summer, sit outside and enjoy the terrace's magnificent view of the Seine, St.Gervais St. Protais Church and Notre Dame!
Hours: Monday - Sunday for lunch (12:00 pm - 2:30 pm) and dinner (7:00 pm - 11:30 pm).
Price Range: €21 - €40
Closest Subway Station: Pont Marie
Address: 1 Rue du Pont Louis-Philippe, 75004 Paris

7. Benoît

Dating back to 1912, Benoit was once ran by a family for three generations but is now run by Alain Ducasse, who has revamped this restaurant into an elegant dining experience. If you have a picture in your head of a golden age of Parisian dining, it probably looks something like Benoit: brass fixtures, lace curtains, velvet banquettes, and a polished zinc bar. The menu offers your traditional elegant French favorites. If you do not want to spend a fortune, come for lunch, as Benoit offers a fixed-priced menu for only 38 euros, which is totally affordable for fancy dining.

Hours: Monday - Sunday for lunch (12:00 pm - 2:30 pm) and dinner (7:00 pm - 11:30 pm).
Price Range: €39 to €106
Closest Subway Station: Hôtel de Ville
Address: 20 Rue Saint-Martin, 75004 Paris

8. Mon Vieil Ami

Run by acclaimed Alsatian (Northeastern France) chef Antoine Westermann, Mon Vieil Ami will allow you to taste amazing Alsatian dishes that rotate seasonally. The menu includes: pâté en croute (wrapped in pastry) and pork pot-au-feu (meaning "pot on the fire"), a traditional stew served with horseradish. You can also try some Alsatian wine. Inside, you will find yourself in a cool, updated medieval dining room with stone walls and dark wood tables.

Hours: Wednesday - Sunday for lunch (12:00 pm - 2:30 pm) and dinner (7:00 pm - 11:00 pm). Closed Monday and Tuesday.
Price Range: €20 - €61
Closest Subway Station: Pont Marie (7)
Address: 69 Rue Saint-Louis en l'Île, 75004 Paris

9. L'As Du Falafel

In the historically Marais neighborhood of Paris, although there are a plethora of falafel stands, you can distinguish the best of the best by the presence of a long line snaking along the street. L'As Du Falafel ("the Ace of Falafel") is a favorite among Parisians because of its one-of-a-kind falafel sandwich, which includes grilled eggplant, cabbage, hummus, tahini, and hot sauce. Yum! Join the line for a delicious sandwich -- it moves fast -- or take a seat at a table and peruse other menu options like chicken shawarma and lamb kabobs.

Opening Hours: Monday - Thursday (12:00 pm - 11:00 pm), Friday (12:00 pm - 4:00 pm), Saturday (6:30 pm - 11:00 pm), and Sunday (12:00 pm - 11:00 pm).
Price Range: €5 - €7.5
Closest Subway Station: Saint-Paul
Address: 32-34 Rue des Rosiers, 75004 Paris

10. Au Bourguignon Du Marais

The name of this restaurant refers to the outstanding regional dishes from Burgundy that are served here. You will find options like snails with garlic and parsley, mustard veal kidneys, foie gras, and, for starters, the boeuf bourguignon. The restaurant also offers a great selection of wines from Burgundy to compliment your delicious meal.

Hours: Tuesday - Thursday (12:00 pm - 11:00 pm), Friday - Saturday (12:00 pm - 11:30 pm). Closed Sunday and Monday.
Price Range: €8 - €20
Closest Subway Station: Pont Marie
Address: 52 Rue François Miron, 75004 Paris

10 Best Restaurants for 5th Arrondissement:

The 5ᵗʰ Arrondissement is located on the left bank (rive gauche), which provides a great view of Notre Dame and is in close proximity to the Luxembourg Gardens. The 5ᵗʰ Arrondissement is known as the Latin Quarter because the Sorbonne, where students studied Latin at one time, is in this area. A colorful neighborhood, the Latin Quarter is made up of winding cobblestone streets lined with little shops and restaurants.

1.   Brasserie Balzar

One of the last brasseries in the Latin Quarter, Brasserie Balzar has been carrying on the great tradition of Parisian brasseries since 1886. The restaurant attracts politicians, writers, tourists, and tons of locals. Regulars frequent Brasserie Balzar because the food is precise and tasty, the service is attentive and sometimes wry, and the owner is very cordial.

Hours: Monday - Sunday for lunch and dinner (11:30 am - 11:30 pm).
Price Range: €21 - €40
Closest Subway Station: Cluny - La Sorbonne
Address: 49 Rue des Écoles, 75005 Paris

2.   L'Atelier Maitre Albert

This restaurant has an ever-changing menu designed by Michelin star chef Guy Savoy, so you cannot go wrong! L'Atelier Maitre Albert is an authentic upscale rotisserie just a stone's throw away from the Notre Dame cathedral. Inside, you will find yourself in an elegantly formal dining room that is warmed by the hearth and full of pleasant aromas from the rotisserie.

Hours: Monday - Wednesday for lunch (12:00 pm - 2:30 pm) and dinner (6:30 pm - 11:00 pm); Thursday and Friday for lunch (12:00 pm - 2:30 pm) and dinner (6:30 pm - 1:00 am); Saturday dinner only (6:30 pm - 1:00 am); Sunday dinner only (6:30 pm - 11:00 pm).
Price Range: €21 - €40
Closest Subway Station: Maubert - Mutualité
Address: 1 Rue Maître Albert, 75005 Paris

3.   Le Petit Prince

This restaurant, on the site of a former 15th-century inn, has a charming and cozy ambiance and is a well-known night spot. Le Petit Prince offers flavorsome traditional French cuisine with a menu that changes by the season to guarantee new flavors. This place will take you back in time to discover old Paris and its warm authenticity.

Hours: Monday - Sunday (7:30 pm - 2:00 am)
Price Range: €8 - €20
Closest Subway Station: Maubert - Mutualité
Address: 12 Rue de Lanneau, 75005 Paris

4.   Les Papilles

Les Papilles ("taste buds") is a classic French bistro that also serves as a wine shop and delicatessen. The kitchen prepares a single menu daily that depends on what Chef Ulric Claude finds at the market that day. The terrific selection of wines is displayed alongside open shelving where customers can browse and choose. You definitely will not be disappointed with this joint!

Hours: Tuesday - Saturday (9:00 am - 1:00 am). Closed Sunday and Monday.
Price Range: €10 - €40
Closest Subway Station: Luxembourg (RER B)
Address: 30 Rue Gay-Lussac, 75005 Paris

5. Chez René

Open since the 1950s, Chez Rene is a perfect representation of the classic Parisian bistro. Serving staples of French cuisine like beef stew, chicken cooked in wine, and calf kidneys, it is adorned with crisp white tablecloths on every table, burgundy woodwork, a zinc-covered bar, and photos of the staff from every decade since the '50s.

Hours: Tuesday - Saturday for lunch (12:00 pm - 2:30 pm) and dinner (7:00 pm - 11:00 pm). Closed Sunday and Monday.
Price Range: €21 - €40
Closest Subway Station: Maubert-Mutualité ou Jussieu
Address: 14 Boulevard Saint-Germain, 75005 Paris

6. Pré Verre

Pré Verre offers delicious traditional French cuisine with a rather "nouvelle" twist -- lighter, more delicate dishes with an emphasis on presentation. You can enjoy an excellent three-course meal with a good bottle of wine and an aperitif, all for an affordable price. Recently remodeled, the interior now displays very attractive decor.

Hours: Tuesday - Saturday for lunch (12:00 pm - 2:00 pm) and dinner (7:30 pm - 10:30 pm). Closed Sunday and Monday.
Price Range: €10 - €40
Closest Subway Station: Cluny La Sorbonne (10)
Address: 8 Rue Thénard, 75005 Paris

7. La Brouette

If you are looking for a reasonably priced and incredibly delicious meal, this is a good spot. Here, you will find three different menus with three different prices (from least to moderately expensive), and the middle-priced menu seems to be the best bang for your buck. It boasts a cozy atmosphere, good service, and a cool terrace; come here if you are looking to save some bucks and eat a great meal at the same time.

Hours: Monday - Sunday, (12:00 pm – 1:00 am)
Price Range: €21 - €40
Closest Subway Station: Cardinal Lemoine
Address: 41 Rue Descartes, 75005 Paris

8. Itinéraires

After the great success of their original restaurant in the 11th Arrondissement, Sylvain and Sarah Sendra decided to upgrade and open up Itineraires in the Latin Quarter. The restaurant is a modern day bistro that will make you step out of your comfort zone to try some of the most interesting and delicious mixes of flavors; the meals are truly pieces of artwork on your plate. Inside, you will find a softly lit room brightened with palm trees and flowers, and chic couples of all ages.

Hours: Tuesday - Saturday for lunch (12:00 pm - 2:30 pm) and dinner (8:00 pm - 11:30 pm). Closed Sunday and Monday.
Price Range: €20 - €100
Closest Subway Station: Maubert-Mutualité (10)
Address: 5 Rue de Pontoise, 75005 Paris

9. L'Agrume

Opened in 2010 by Chef Franck Marchesi-Grandi (ex-chef from Le Bernardin in New York), L'Agrume is a very small restaurant where the chef is cooking his heart out in a small, open kitchen. Since it is a super small restaurant, snagging a table can be tough, so reserve one ahead of time. Lunch is a great value and definitely a gourmet experience. In the evening, expect to try an exquisite, no-choice degustation of five courses which changes every day.

Hours: Tuesday - Saturday for lunch (12:00 pm - 2:30 pm) and dinner (7:00 pm - 10:30 pm). Closed Sunday and Monday.
Price Range: €8 - €40
Closest Subway Station: Les Gobelins (7) or St. Marcel (5)
Address: 15 Rue des Fossés St-Marcel, 75005 Paris

10. Le Bistro des Gastronomes

Offering delicious contemporary bistro cooking, Le Bistro des Gastronomes is super affordable. Inside, the dining room is rather simple and austere, but the service is very friendly and the chef creates great dishes, most of which are based on his family's favorite meals.

Hours: Tuesday - Saturday for lunch (12:00 pm - 2:30 pm) and dinner (7:00 pm - 11:00 pm). Closed Sunday and Monday.
Price Range: €21 - €50
Closest Subway Station: Cardinal Lemoine (10)
Address: 10 Rue du Cardinal Lemoine, 75005 Paris

10 Best Restaurants for 6th Arrondissement:

The 6th Arrondissement, also known as St. Germain de Pres, is a colorful part of the Left Bank that was once the favorite hangout spot of writer Ernest Hemingway and the artist Delacroix. Today you can stroll the famous Boulevard St Germain, or find the former homes of famous authors on rue Jacob. The beautiful Luxembourg Gardens can be found here as well.

1. Le Comptoir du Relais

Le comptoir du Relais only seats 20 -- yup, only 20! So reservations are a must and should be made several months in advance for dinner. The single five-course fixed-priced-menu dinner allows Chef Yves Camdeborde to take real pleasure in his work, which is very inventive and surprising. Fortunately, if you cannot get a table for the evening, Le Comptoir also functions as a more casual brasserie during lunchtime. The art deco dining room has blue and yellow tile floors, white-clothed tables, and a large mirror displaying handwritten daily specials.

Hours: Monday - Friday for lunch and dinner (12:00 pm - 12:00 am), Saturday for lunch only (12:00 pm - 2:00 pm), and Sunday for lunch and dinner (12:00 pm - 11:00 pm).
Price Range: €20 - €49
Closest Subway Station: Odéon (4, 10)
Address: 9 Carrefour de l'Odéon, 75006 Paris

2. L'Epi Dupin

Chef Francois Pasteau has developed an incredibly popular "bistronomic' (bistro + gastronomic) concept that makes this place a foodie's paradise. Here, it is all about the fresh ingredients and using haute cuisine techniques when cooking up hearty classic dishes that change often. At L'Epi Dupin, step out of your comfort zone -- you will not be disappointed! Make reservations in advance, as this is a true hot spot location.

Hours: Monday for dinner only (7:00 pm - 10:30 pm), Tuesday - Friday for lunch (12:00 pm - 2:30 pm) and dinner (7:00 pm - 10:30 pm). Closed Saturday and Sunday.
Price Range: €8 - €50
Closest Subway Station: Sevres-Babylone (10, 12)
Address: 11 Rue Dupin, 75006 Paris

3. Les Editeurs

A lounge bar, a restaurant, a tea room, and a library, all in one - how cool is that! At Les Editeurs, there are over 5,000 books you can choose from to read while you enjoy a cup of coffee. Or, you can have a great lunch with a glass of wine or a snack. It is a nice break from a traditional restaurant setting. This is a super hip but comfortable place to hang out for a few hours during your day.

Hours: Monday - Sunday (8:00 am - 2:00 am).
Price Range: €21 - €40
Closest Subway Station: Odéon
Address: 4 Carrefour de l'Odéon, 75006 Paris

4.   La Rotonde

An extensive menu with generous portions makes this a great place for everyone. A true value in Paris, the atmosphere is casual and the location is very popular, as it is in a great neighborhood, which is perfect for people watching. Since 1911, it has been a popular place for artists and filmmakers to frequent. Artists such as Pablo Picasso frequented this joint!

Hours: Monday - Sunday (8:00 am - 2:00 am).
Price Range: €20 - €50
Closest Subway Station: Vavin (4)
Address: 105 Boulevard du Montparnasse, 75006 Paris

5.   La Ferrandaise

The chef at La Ferrandaise makes it his mission to serve local gourmet cuisine. Here, you will discover local products like veal Auvergne Ferrandais or Auvergne cheeses, but you will also rediscover "pub food" like traditional veal stew, the Burgundian beef, and seafood. Each menu is accompanied by seasonal organic vegetables and a wine list of small and large producers of the French vineyards. All of the products offered at La Ferrandiase (including wines) are carefully selected for their quality and freshness, and they focus as much as possible on organic producers.

Hours: Monday (7:00 pm - 10:30 pm), Tuesday - Friday (12:00 pm - 10:30 pm), and Saturday (7:00 pm - 10:30 pm). Closed Sunday.
Price Range: €21 - €40
Closest Subway Station: Odéon
Address: 8 Rue de Vaugirard, 75006 Paris

6.   Sud-Ouest & Cie

Serving dishes that specialize in traditional Southwestern cuisine, Sud-Ouest & Cie is an inviting restaurant with a great "homey" atmosphere. Its most famous and popular dish is definitely duck with confit and foie gras.

Hours: Monday - Thursday (12:00 am - 10:30 pm), Friday and Saturday (12:00 am - 11:00 pm), and Sunday (12:00 am - 10:30 pm)
Price Range: €21 - €40
Closest Subway Station: Montparnasse - Bienvenüe
Address: 39 Boulevard du Montparnasse, 75006 Paris

7.   Le Rousseau

Like any restaurant named after a famous philosopher should be, Le Rousseau is a thoughtful and inspired brasserie. Very comfortable and trendy, this place is lively and fun as well. It has a welcoming setting and serves traditional cuisine that you will definitely enjoy.

Hours: Monday - Saturday (8:00 am - 12:00 am). Closed Sunday.
Price Range: €21 - €40

Closest Subway Station: Rennes
Address: 45 Rue du Cherche-Midi, 75006 Paris

8. L'Alcazar

You can easily walk past this place and not realize it is, in fact, a restaurant, as there are no chairs outside and no diners in the window seats. When you enter, first impressions are as though you are entering a Paris nightclub, not a restaurant. Chic, fun, trendy, and comfortable, this popular restaurant was designed by Sir Terence Conran. You will enjoy a range of options from seafood to classic French and English inspired dishes. There is modern art and photography displayed on the walls and classy, friendly service to go with the stylish decor.

Hours: Monday - Sunday for lunch (12:00 pm - 2:30 pm) and dinner (7:00 pm - 11:30 pm).
Price Range: €11 - €40
Closest Subway Station: Mabillon
Address: 62 Rue Mazarine, 75006 Paris

9. Polidor

A historic restaurant in Paris, the Cremerie restaurant Polidor was founded in 1845. Here, you will feel as if you are stepping back in time -- the interior of the restaurant seems to have not been touched for over 100 years, sending you straight to the 19th-century. Offering traditional French cuisine, this place is extremely popular and crowded. It is definitely one of those places that you will be telling your friends about when you return home!

Hours: Monday - Saturday for lunch (12:00 pm - 2:30 pm) and dinner (7:00 pm - 12:30 am), Sunday for lunch (12:00 pm - 2:30 pm) and dinner (7:00 pm - 11:00 pm).
Price Range: €8 - €20
Closest Subway Station: Odéon
Address: 41 Rue Monsieur le Prince, 75006 Paris

10. Casa Bini

If you are tired of French food, or simply want to mix things up, try Casa Bini. Casa Bini looks like a rustic taverna and serves excellent Italian food that changes often to take advantage of fresh seafood and seasonal produce. Pastas are homemade daily here, but what Casa Bini is best known for is its various selections of delicious carpaccio. You definitely will not be disappointed here.

Hours: Tuesday - Saturday for lunch (12:30 pm - 2:30 pm) and dinner (7:30 pm - 11:00 pm). Closed Sunday and Monday.
Price Range: €21 - €40
Closest Subway: Mabillon
Address: 36 Rue Grégoire de Tours, 75006 Paris

10 Best Restaurants for 7th Arrondissement:

The 7th Arrondissement is known as St-Germain-des-Pres because the church of that name is a landmark in this area. Great for shopping and eating, this area is lively and lovely. In the 7th you will find anything from Michelin-starred restaurants to great hole-in-the-wall cafes.

1. Le Violon d'Ingres

Owned by renowned chef Christian Constant, Le Violon d'Ingres was formerly a Michelin star restaurant, but in 2006, he decided to give up his star and turn his fancy and expensive restaurant into an inviting and enjoyable restaurant more accessible to the masses. Moderately-priced, you can choose three courses from a rather varied menu to create your own menu. Whatever you choose, you will not be disappointed since the portions are bigger than average, as are the flavors.

Hours: Monday - Sunday for lunch (12:00 pm - 2:30 pm) and dinner (7:00 pm - 10:30 pm).
Price Range: €49 - €95
Closest Subway: École Militaire
Address: 135 Rue Saint-Dominique, 75007 Paris

2. Café Constant

Another one of Chef Christian Constant's restaurants, Cafe Constant is a postcard of what a classic Parisian bistro looks like. It is a casual restaurant that features excellent food at reasonable prices and an ever-changing seasonal menu. With a no-reservation policy, it is understandably packed during peak meal times, so come early or later to get the best spots available.

Hours: Monday - Sunday for lunch and dinner (7:00 am - 11:00 pm).
Price Range: €21 - €40
Closest Subway: École Militaire (8) or Pont de l'Alma (RER C)
Address: 139 Rue Saint-Dominique, 75007 Paris

3. Au Petit Sud Ouest

The name of this restaurant literally translates to "small southwest," and it specializes in everything duck-related. Au Petit Sud Ouest is most popular for offering its guests an extensive foie gras selection, magret de canard, and confit de canard. The restaurant interior is like that of a rustic countryside and the dishes seem to reinforce this theme. Here, you are sure to have a charming dining experience.

Hours: Tuesday - Saturday for lunch (12:00 pm - 2:00 pm) and dinner (6:00 pm - 10:00 pm). Closed Sunday and Monday.
Price Range: €21 - €40
Closest Subway: École Militaire
Address: 46 Avenue de la Bourdonnais, 75007 Paris

4.   Les Fables de la Fontaine

Another one of Chef Christian Constant's restaurants, this one is the fanciest of them all. This small but charming restaurant offers incredible seafood as its specialty. Having won a Michelin star, this is the priciest restaurant of the Constant Empire. Make your reservations early.

Hours: Monday - Sunday for lunch (12:30 pm - 2:30 pm) and dinner (7:30 pm to 10:30 pm).
Price Range: €21 - €100
Closest Subway: École Militaire (8)
Address: 131 Rue Saint-Dominique, 75007 Paris

5. Thoumieux Restaurant

This one is a super cool, retro, '60s lounge-style dining room, serving 21st-century French gastronomy. Cushy, colorful sofas and chairs, low lighting, cream walls, thick carpeting, and seating for only 20 makes you feel like you are in a private club. This two-Michelin star place is a fusion of brasserie and gastronomical restaurant, as well as a hotel and a space dedicated to the chef's famous pastries! A must for a true Parisian luxury experience.

Hours: Monday - Sunday for lunch and dinner (12:00 pm - 12:00 am).
Price Range: €21 - €50
Closest Subway: La Tour Maubourg (8)
Address: 79 Rue Saint-Dominique, 75007 Paris

6.   Chez L'Ami Jean

Run by celebrated chef Stéphane Jego, this restaurant serves authentic Basque food in a traditional bistro-style setting with tightly packed tables and an open kitchen. Basque sports memorabilia decorate the walls of Chez L'Ami Jean, while strings of garlic and peppers hang from the ceiling. Bread is served with a sealed tin of herbed white cheese, followed by entrées such as braised duck foie gras and homemade desserts like the famous rice pudding with pralines and dried apricots -- yum!

Hours: Tuesday - Saturday for lunch (12:00 pm - 1:30 pm) and dinner (7:00 pm - 9:00 pm). Closed Sunday and Monday.
Price Range: €41 - €100
Closest Subway: La Tour Maubourg (8)
Address: 27 Rue Malar, 75007 Paris

7. La Frégate

A nautically-themed Parisian bistro named after the frigate which docked under Le Pont Royal in the 1870's Commune era, La Frégate has frescoed ceilings and painted pillars that add to the atmosphere. Serving traditional French food, this place is perfect to stop by for a relaxed lunch or a refined dinner.

Hours: Monday - Friday for lunch (12:00 pm - 2:30 pm) and dinner (7:00 pm - 10:30 pm). Closed Saturday and Sunday.
Price Range: €21 - €40
Closest Subway: Mabillon

Address: 1 Rue du Bac, 75007 Paris

8. Le Jules Verne

Located on the 2nd floor of the Eiffel Tower, this Michelin star restaurant offers its guests an incredible view of Paris along with contemporary and accessible French cuisine. One of Alain Ducasse's excellent restaurants, Le Jules Verne will be one of your warmest and most intimate dining experiences in Paris.

Hours: Monday - Sunday (9:00 am - 5:00 pm) and (7:00 pm - 9:00 pm). Closed Sunday and Monday.
Price Range: €190 - €230
Closest Subway: Bir-Hakeim
Address: Tour Eiffel, Avenue Gustave Eiffel, 75007 Paris

9. Aux Fins Gourmets

At Aux Fins Gourmets, enjoy authentic and tasty dishes made with quality ingredients served in an intimate setting. The high ceilings, pale yellow walls, white tablecloths, and well-dressed servers have changed little in the bistro's 50-plus years running, and the restaurant maintains a loyal following of locals. Duck dishes and cassoulet are favorites at this bistro.

Hours: Monday - Saturday for lunch (12:00 pm - 2:30 pm) and dinner (7:00 pm - 10:30 pm). Closed Sunday.
Price Range: €21 - €40
Closest Subway: Ru du Bac
Address: 213 Boulevard Saint-Germain, 75007 Paris

10. La Fontaine de Mars

With its old-fashioned flair, traditional food, and reasonable prices, La Fontaine de Mars is sure to woo you. This restaurant has been around for over 100 years and serves delicious southwestern food. With over 100 years under its belt, you can be sure the restaurant has perfected its menu items.

Hours: Monday - Sunday (12:00 pm - 11:00 pm).
Price Range: €21 - €50
Closest Subway: École Militaire (8)
Address: 129 Rue Saint-Dominique, 75007 Paris

10 Best Restaurants for 8th Arrondissement:

The expensive 8th arrondissement is located on the Right Bank (rive droit), and hugs the beautiful Champs Elysees. Most of the best hotels in Paris are found here, as well as the most famous couturiers and "Grands Magasins" (department stores). The 8th also offers the largest grouping of celebrity chefs in one district. This is Paris at its most chic.

1. La Fermette Marbeuf

Dating back to 1989, this restaurant was rediscovered only 30 years ago during a renovation. Definitely an interesting place to visit and eat, La Fermette Marbeuf is considered a real art Nouveau gem and is listed as a historical monument. Foodies and celebrities from all over come here to enjoy both modern and classic French dishes.

Hours: Monday - Sunday for lunch (12:00 pm - 3:00 pm) and dinner (7:00 pm - 11:30 pm).
Price Range: €45 - €80
Closest Subway: Alma - Marceau
Address: 5 Rue Marbeuf, 75008 Paris

2. Citrus Étoile

The youngest chef to ever win a Michelin star, Chef Gilles Epie is the 22 year old owner of this spectacular restaurant. Renowned from Japan to Los Angeles, he returned to Paris with his American wife and opened Citrus Etoile, where he has brought all the freshness, innovation, and style of the City of Angels. The dining space is light and airy with shades of bright orange, sunlight, and fresh flowers. The neo-Californian menu features no fat and little sauce, and it changes constantly, though it retains the "greatest hits," of course.

Hours: Monday - Friday (12:00 pm - 10:30 pm). Closed Saturday and Sunday.
Price Range: €50 - €100
Closest Subway: Citrus Étoile
Address: 6 Rue Arsène Houssaye, 75008 Paris

3. Mini Palais

There is nothing small about Le Mini Palais. Upon entering through the massive bronze door, the vast, high-ceilinged room makes you feel like you are in a classy artist's loft with its floor to ceiling windows, metal support beams painted green, and strategically-placed mirrors that create an illusion of expansiveness. Not to mention that outside, there is an incredible terrace with imperial columns and mosaics on the walls and floors, making it the most splendid in the city. Serving cosmopolitan, high-quality, seasonal cuisine, you definitely will not be disappointed.

Hours: Sunday - Saturday (10:00 am - 2:00 am)
Price Range: €21 - €50
Closest Subway: Champs-Elysées Clemenceau (1, 13)
Address: 3 Avenue Winston Churchill, 75008 Paris

4. Lazare

A train station might seem like a peculiar venue for a seriously good restaurant. However, tucked away in the shopping mall of the Saint-Lazare train station is one of the best, owned by the Hotel Bristol's 3-star chef, Eric Frechon. Lazare is divided into multiple sections: a delicatessen, a huge wooden table, a bar and a lounge to sip a drink, and the great dining room - designed in the style of a kitchen with tableware stored in cupboards all along the walls. It is a bustling modern brasserie concept with old world touches that is open throughout the day for breakfast, lunch, tea and dinner.

Hours: Sunday - Saturday (7:30 am - 12:00 am)
Price Range: €21 - €60
Closest Subway: Saint-Lazare (3,12,13,14)
Address: Parvis de la Gare Saint-Lazare, Rue Intérieure, 75008 Paris

5. Restaurant Dominique Bouchet

Chef Dominique Bouchet is known for his more upscale restaurants, La Tour d'Argent and Hotel de Crillon. However, at his self-named bistro, he embraces simpler and less pricey fare for the masses. With only 40 seats, reservations are recommended, and you will find yourself surrounded by stone walls, ebony woods, and low lighting. The small menu features traditional French entrees, home-style desserts, and some great wine.

Hours: Monday - Friday for lunch (12:00 pm - 2:00 pm) and dinner (7:30 pm - 9:30 pm). Closed Saturday and Sunday.
Price Range: €8 - €20
Closest Subway: Miromesnil
Address: 11 Rue Treilhard, 75008 Paris

6. Le 68 Guy Martin

When you enter the famous Guerlain perfume store on the Champs-Elysees, you are not likely to think that downstairs in its "basement," hiding from view, is an elegant restaurant and tea salon. When gastronomy meets the world of perfume, it is all about taste and flair. Beyond the combination of these two universes, this place welcomes you warmly for a multi-sensorial experience. Amazing and talented chef Guy Martin took one year to create a surprising and exciting menu based on the Guerlain fragrances.

Hours: Sunday - Saturday (10:00 am - 11:00 pm)
Price Range: €11 - €40
Closest Subway: Ligne n°1 & 9 - FRANKLIN D. ROOSEVELT
Address: 68 Av. des Champs-Élysées, 75008 Paris

7. Neva Cuisine

Mexican-born chef Beatriz Gonzalez's restaurant Neva Cuisine has become a hit destination, thanks to her astounding contemporary French cooking. With its elegant, simple, and modern furnishings, high ceilings, and 19th-century-style glass-ball chandeliers, Neva Cuisine is something of an anomaly in the neighborhood, but the food is to die for.

Hours: Monday - Friday for lunch (12:30 pm - 2:00 pm) and dinner (7:00 pm - 10:00 pm), Saturday (7:00 pm - 10:00 pm). Closed Sunday.
Price Range: €21 - €50
Closest Subway: Europe (3) or Liège (13)
Address: 2 Rue de Berne, 75008 Paris

8.   L'Instant d'Or

Just off the Champs-Elysées, this luxury brasserie is comprised of three refined rooms: The first dining room features an incredible chandelier by Géraud de Torsiac; the second is decked out in sensual red velvet; and the third, being the most luxurious, is decorated with embroidered satin and Toile de Jouy motifs. The talented chef Frederic Duca creates French regional cuisine to perfection.
Hours: Tuesday - Saturday for lunch (12:30pm - 2:30pm) and dinner (7:30pm-22:30pm). Closed Sunday and Monday.
Price Range: €41 - €100
Closest Subway: George V (1)
Address: 36 Avenue George V, 75008 Paris

9.   Les Elysees

In the 4-star Hotel Vernet, you willl find Les Elysees, a restaurant in a century-old room with a stained glass dome. Boasting one Michelin star, Chef Eric Biffard serves wonderful, seasonal, modern French cuisine with exotic touches. Also, the wine cellar contains more than 12,000 bottles, covering more than 900 types of wine!

Hours: Monday - Friday for lunch (12:00 pm - 2:00 pm) and dinner (7:30 pm - 11:00 pm), Saturday (7:30 pm - 11:00 pm). Closed Sunday.
Price Range: €15 - €50
Closest Subway: Charles de Gaulle Etoile
Address: 25 Rue Vernet, 75008 Paris

10. Alain Ducasse au Plaza Athénée

Located at the ritzy Hotel Plaza Athenee is Alain Ducasse's 3-Michelin star restaurant. Even pricey by Parisian standards, here you will try incredible haute cuisine with designer decor. After celebrating their 10-year anniversary, the restaurant has embraced a simpler menu favoring fewer ingredients, less salt, and less fat content. Table art adorns a luxurious dining room backed by a series of exquisitely embroidered screens.

Hours: Thursday and Friday for lunch (12:45 am - 2:15 pm), Monday - Friday for dinner (7:30 pm - 10:15 pm).
Price Range: €41 - €100 and above
Closest Subway: Alma - Marceau
Address: Alain Ducasse au Plaza Athénée

10 Best Restaurants for 9th Arrondissement:

Known locally as "SoPi" (South Pigalle) Paris' active working class 9th Arrondissement, just east of the Opera Garnier and north of the Grands Boulevards, is an adventure for most first-time visitors. The recent explosion of bistros, neo-bistros, diners, tapas, wine bars, and French versions of American classics such as hotdogs, burgers, and cocktails make the 9th Arrondissement a great place to dine.

1. Le Vaisseau Vert

Le Vaisseau Vert is great for those special nights when you want an elegant and unique dining experience. The place boasts a good combination of contemporary art and inventive French-Japanese influence on the menu. It is a definite must-try.
Hours: Tuesday - Friday (12:30 pm - 2:30 pm), Tuesday - Saturday (7:30 pm - 10:30 pm)
Price Range: €50 - €80
Closest Subway: Liège
Address: 10 rue de Parme, 75009 Paris

2. Le Flamboire

If you love long-braised and barbecued meats, this is definitely the place for you. One of the only "flamboires" in town, here you will find interesting decor with a huge and stunning chimney as a backdrop and flames painted on the walls. In front, you will find the chef cooking a carnivorous meal in a wood-burning oven. And for those who do not eat red meat, fish is also an option.

Hours: Monday - Saturday for lunch (12:00 pm - 3:00 pm) and dinner (6:30 pm - 11:00 pm). Closed Sunday.
Price Range: €41 - €78
Closest Subway: Liège
Address: 54 Rue Blanche, 75009 Paris

3. L'Office

In a neighborhood not known for its bistros, L'Office is a restaurant through which owner Chef Nicolas Sheidt is aiming to change just that. The place is decorated with big mirrors and hanging lights, giving the restaurant a modern spirit, just like the food it serves. The delicious dishes vary with the seasons and are great value for your money.

Hours: Monday - Friday for lunch (12:00 pm - 2:00 pm) and dinner (7:30 pm - 10:30 pm). Closed Saturday and Sunday.
Price Range: €21 - €40
Closest Subway: Cadet (7)
Address: 3 Rue Richer, 75009 Paris

4. Hotel Amour

This hotel's restaurant, bar, and charming interior terrace serves as the Paris go-to spot for hipsters and some of the hottest names in fashion and art. Designed with a 1950's decor, you are considered lucky to get a spot to sit outside on the terrace. Unlike many Parisian restaurants that offer fixed priced menus, Hotel Amour's menu is a la carte, and although the food is good, you will come here for the atmosphere, as it is super hip and cool.

Hours: Open every day, Monday - Sunday (8:00 am - 12:00 am).
Price Range: €20 - €40
Closest Subway: Pigalle (2, 12) or Saint-Georges (12)
Address: 8 Rue Navarin, 75009 Paris

5. Le Garde-Temps

The chalkboard menus of this contemporary bistro are framed and hung on the walls, and, thankfully, the promise of gastronomic art does not disappoint. Older style bistro standards are slowly disappearing and more imaginative standards in bistros are becoming common. However, unlike the new bistros, here at Le Garde-Temps, you will not need to pay an arm and a leg to eat. They even have an extensive wine list. Truly an utter delight!

Hours: Monday - Saturday for lunch (12:30 pm - 2:00 pm) and dinner (7:00 pm - 11:30 pm). Closed Sunday.
Price Range: €20 - €40
Closest Subway: Pigalle (2, 12)
Address: 19bis Rue Pierre Fontaine, 75009 Paris

6. Le Pantruche

An old slang word for "Parisian," Le Pantruche has a seasonal bistro fare, reasonable prices, and an intimate setting. The menu includes everything from classics (steak with béarnaise sauce) to more daring creations (scallops served in a parmesan broth with cauliflower mousseline), all at affordable prices. With classic bistro decor, myriad mirrors, a smiling staff, and great food, you are sure to leave happy.
Hours: Monday - Friday for lunch (12:30 pm - 2:00 pm) and dinner (7:00 pm - 11:30 pm). Closed Sunday.
Price Range: €20 - €40
Closest Subway: Pigalle (2, 12)
Address: 3 Rue Victor Masse, 75009 Paris

7. Buvette

A replica of her restaurant in New York, American chef Jody Williams has impressed Parisians with her beautiful restaurant that serves delicious French food. She dubbed her restaurants "gastrotheques"- a word she invented to describe both its informality and its delightfulness. Fresh ingredients are bought in from local bio producers, and the menu changes seasonally. The portions are meant to be shared among friends. There is also an extensive wine list. There are no reservations, so come early, or come really late.

Hours: Monday - Friday (8:30 am - 12:00 am), Saturday and Sunday (10:30 am - 12:30 am).
Price Range: €8 - €40
Closest Subway: Pigalle (2, 12), Saint-Georges (12)
Address: 28 Rue Henry Monnier, 75009 Paris

8.   Petrelle

Petrelle is an extremely small and cozy restaurant. Decorated with Victorian candlesticks, beautiful paintings, chandeliers, and a house cat and dog that roam the restaurant, Petrelle makes you feel like you are at home. With only one waiter, one cook, and one busser, you can imagine just how small it really is. New French dishes are served here a la carte, and the menu changes with the season. It is not exactly cheap, and there are not a lot of menu options, but do not worry -- they are all absolutely delicious!

Hours: Tuesday - Saturday (8:00 pm - 9:30 pm). Closed Sunday and Monday.
Price Range: €50 - €100
Closest Subway: Anvers
Address: 34 Rue Petrelle, 75009 Paris

9. Le Laffitte

Established in 1913, Le Laffitte serves familiar and traditional French cuisine in generous portions. With paper tablecloths over red-and-white checked cotton ones, blackboards displaying the specials of the day, and fruit tarts cooling on the bar, this place makes you feel very traditionally Parisian. If you are tired of "fashion food" and just want to eat a real meal like grandmother's cooking, this is the spot to go.

Hours: Monday - Friday (7:00 am - 9:00 pm). Closed Saturday and Sunday.
Price Range: €20 - €40
Closest Subway: Notre-Dame-de-Lorette
Address: 43 Rue Laffitte, 75009 Paris

10. L'Opéra Restaurant

Inside one of Paris's most cherished monuments (the Opera House), L'Opera Restaurant makes you feel as if you have stepped into the future, along with being visually stunning. Food-wise, you can expect to eat incredibly flavorsome dishes with influences from all over the world. Come here during opera season, before or after your show.

Hours: Monday - Sunday (7:00 am - 12:00 am).
Price Range: €20 - €40
Closest Subway: Chaussée d'Antin
Address: Palais Garnier, 1 Place Jacques Rouché, 75009 Paris

10 Best Restaurants for 10th Arrondissement:

The 10ᵗʰ Arrondissement centers around the Canal St. Martin and the restaurants and cafés which line its banks. The two great train stations, Gare du Nord and Gare de l'Estare, are located here. The 10ᵗʰ Arrondissement is home to some of the best multi-cultural restaurants in Paris, offering a wide range of restaurants, cafes, and bistros to suit every budget.

1.   Abri

On Mondays and Saturdays from 10 am to 5 pm, this is the place to be! Only on these days can you try their multi-layered, super stacked, millfueille-esque sandwiches, put together by the young Japanese chef, Katsuaki Okiyama. Of course, on other days there are plenty more of this young chef's creations to choose from that are French cuisine with Japanese touches. Because it is super-small, you will need to make a reservation weeks, even months, in advance.

Hours: Monday - Saturday (11:45 am - 10:00 pm). Closed Sunday.
Price Range: €20 - €50
Closest Subway: Poissonnière (7)
Address: 92 Rue du Faubourg Poissonnière, 75010 Paris

2.   Chez Michel

The food of France's Breton region shines at this charming little restaurant, located in the chef's hometown. Chez Michel is a haven for foodies everywhere, as chef Thierry Breton's menu is known for both fresh Breton seafood as well as his use of obscure ingredients. The exterior is rather simple, but that is because the staff has concentrated more on the quality of the food than on the decor.

Hours: Monday (7:00 pm - 12:00 am), Tuesday - Friday (12:00 pm - 2:00 pm) and (7:00 pm - 12:00 am). Closed Saturday and Sunday.
Price Range: €20 - €100
Closest Subway: Poissonière (7)
Address: 10 Rue de Belzunce, 75010 Paris

3.   Il Toscano 0039

This little hole in the wall offers incredibly delicious Tuscan food at affordable prices. Here, you are guaranteed authentic Tuscan food - unpretentious and hearty. Of course pizza is the specialty of the house, and it is to die for. So if you are looking for a little taste of Italy in Paris, this is the place to go.
Hours: Monday - Sunday (12:00 pm - 3:00 pm) and (6:30 pm - 11:00 pm).
Price Range: €9 - €20
Closest Subway: Boissière ligne 6
Address: 128 Rue du Faubourg Saint-Martin, 75010 Paris

4. La Cantine de Quentin

Whether you are stopping in to buy foie gras from the grocery or settling in for a leisurely brunch or lunch overlooking the idyllic Canal Saint Martin, La Cantine de Quentin is a worthy destination. The blackboard menu changes often, and the wood-paneled facade and covered bistro tables out front will remind you of a classic Parisian sidewalk cafe, while the interior walls are decorated with gourmet groceries from the countryside and great French wines. Be sure to end your meal with a dessert here.

Hours: Tuesday - Sunday for lunch only (10:00 am - 7:00 pm).
Price Range: €8 - €30
Closest Subway: Jacques Bonsergent (5)
Address: 52 Rue Bichat, 75010 Paris

5. Le Verre Volé

This tiny place only has room for twenty people at a time, but it is truly a must-visit. Carefully selected bottles of wine from France's wine regions line the walls, and guests can buy bottles to enjoy in the shop or buy by the glass. The knowledgeable staff will help you pick out something in your price range and explain to you the types of great wine available. The menu is handwritten on a chalkboard and changes often. Since seating is limited, reservations are recommended.

Hours: Monday - Sunday for lunch (12:00 pm - 2:30 pm) and dinner (7:30 pm - 11:30 pm).
Price Range: €10 - €40
Closest Subway: Jacques Bonsergent (5)
Address: 67 Rue de Lancry, 75010 Paris

6. Haï Kaï

Having opened in 2014, this place is fairly new and is a must visit spot. Haikai is a satirical Japanese verse form, a salute to the Far Eastern influences which you can detect in the decor and the cooking. The interior is simple but comes to life with lots of beautiful plants. The food tastes as good as it looks. At lunch, the menu is similar to more traditional Parisian standards offering fixed prices; in the evenings, everything is a la carte.

Hours: Tuesday - Saturday for lunch and dinner (12:15 pm - 10:30 pm). Closed Sunday and Monday.
Price Range: €20 - €70
Closest Subway: Jacques Bonsergent (5)
Address: 104 Quai de Jemmapes, 75010 Paris

7. Vivant

Pierre Jancou has a knack for finding locations (three restaurants) and for unearthing buried gems; most would say he does the same thing with food and wine. Jancou's trademark passion for all things natural and organic and the people who produce them is once again on full display at this gorgeous bistro. He finds the best products from passionate farmers, vignerons, and artisans. Vivant is located in a former bird shop, decorated with interesting tile work and painted with peacocks. If you have never tried organic wine before, now is your chance!

Hours: Monday - Friday for lunch (12:00 pm - 2:30 pm) and dinner (7:00 pm - 10:30 pm). Closed Saturday and Sunday.
Price Range: €20 - €100
Closest Subway: Bonne Nouvelle (8, 9)
Address: 43 Rue des Petites Écuries, 75010 Paris

8. La Marine

Set on the corner street across from the Canal St. Martin, La Marine is a classic neighborhood brasserie serving reasonably priced traditional French fare, like the classic boeuf bourguignon. Inside, the brasserie is decorated with red velvet curtains, gold-framed mirrors, intimate tables, and a small zinc bar. Outside seating is also available when the weather permits, allowing for great people watching and a beautiful view of the canal.

Hours: Monday - Sunday (8:00 am - 2:00 am).
Price Range: €8 - €20
Closest Subway: Jacques Bonsergent
Address: 55 Bis Quai de Valmy, 75010 Paris

9. Hôtel du Nord

Inspired by the 1938 Marcel Carne movie of the same name, Hotel du Nord is arguably one of the best cafes in Paris. The decor is traditional Parisian with a green facade, velvet curtains guarding the bar, a sidewalk terrace, and dining tables placed behind bookshelves. Most guests enjoy drinks at the bar, browse through the library upstairs, then enjoy a delicious meal. Here, favorite dishes include the foie gras and duck confit.

Hours: Monday and Sunday only (9:00 am - 1:30 am). Closed Tuesday - Saturday.
Price Range: €21 - €40
Closest Subway: Jacques Bonsergent
Address: 102 Quai de Jemmapes, 75010 Paris

10. ☐Madame Shawn

If you want to explore the richness of Thai gastronomy in Paris, this is your chance. This authentic Thai mini-chain now has seven restaurants in the city, all highly praised by regulars and newcomers alike; however, the mother nest is here in the charming Canal Saint Martin quarter. Decorated with Buddhas, bamboo screens, black wooden chairs, and soft lighting, the peaceful atmosphere is perfect for a meal before or after a walk along the banks of the canal. If you are not into spicy food, do not worry -- the heat can be turned down a few notches, and you will still be able to taste the flavors of Thailand in your meal.

Hours: Monday - Sunday for lunch (12:00 pm - 3:00 pm) and dinner (7:00 pm to 11:00 pm).
Price Range: €21 - €40
Closest Subway: Jacques Bonsergent
Address: 56 rue de Lancry, 75010 Paris, France

10 Best Restaurants for 11th Arrondissement:

The 11th Arrondissement is home to two different but equally blossoming centers of Parisian nightlife. The streets northwest of Place de Bastille are full of small restaurants which attract a mix of young suburban Parisians, expats, and foreigners. Many have a Latin-American theme. The restaurants, bars, and wine bars around Rue Oberkampf north of the 11th and Rue de Charonne near Avenue Ledru Rollin attract a more urban crowd, and the restaurants are perhaps closer to something more traditionally Parisian. The 11th Arrondissement is set near the place de la Republique and the Bastille. It is close to the Marais and is still considered central Paris.

1. Bones Bar & Restaurant

Bones, a trendy restaurant and bar for hipsters and foodies, is run by Australian born chef James Henry. The food is made with the freshest possible ingredients, the wine is a showcase of France's best artisanal and natural selections, and the beer is craft. You can either enter the bar area with no reservation and enjoy a glass of wine and a snack of very fresh oysters, or make a reservation (weeks in advance) to sit in the dining room, where the menu is fixed. Unusual in France, James and his kitchen staff bake bread daily and churn butter, which is absolutely delicious.

Hours: Monday - Sunday for lunch (12:00 pm - 3:00 pm) and dinner (7:00 pm - 11:00 pm).
Price Range: €21 - €40
Closest Subway: Jacques Bonsergent
Address: 43 Rue Godefroy Cavaignac, 75011 Paris

2. La Pulpéria

This Argentinian restaurant by Fernando de Tomaso could more accurately be called a steakeria, given the number and size of steak offerings on their menu. The menu offers a mix of Latin American specialties (ceviche, empanadas, churrasco de la Pampa, etc), but also offers just as many French dishes, which change seasonally. Expect giant portions, plenty of delicious chimichurri, and a great list of wines.

Hours: Monday - Sunday for lunch (12:00 pm - 3:00 pm) and dinner (7:00 pm - 11:00 pm).
Price Range: €21 - €40
Closest Subway: Jacques Bonsergent
Address: 11 Rue Richard Lenoir, 75011 Paris

3. Le 6 Paul Bert

Everything inside this restaurant is set up to make you hungry. Upon entering, you will find a big bar/deli that tempts you with beautiful cheeses and all sorts of charcuterie. Before you reach the restaurant, you will pass by the open kitchen filled with delicious scents and see the cooks hard at work. In the dining room, there is a row of red tables in front of a big picture window. Here, you will be offered a lighter style of French cooking (with smaller portions), and guests can order from a price-fixed menu or a la carte.

Hours: Monday - Sunday for lunch (12:00 pm - 3:00 pm) and dinner (7:00 pm - 11:00 pm).

Price Range: €21 - €40
Closest Subway: Jacques Bonsergent
Address: 6, rue Paul Bert Paris 75011

4. Le Bistrot du Peinture

Le Bistrot du Peinture is a two-story Art Nouveau bistro that has been around since 1902. It is the oldest bistro in the neighborhood, serving authentic French cuisine that changes seasonally. You really cannot go wrong eating here -- the dishes are great, and on sunny days you can sit outside and people-watch.

Hours: Monday - Sunday for lunch (12:00 pm - 3:00 pm) and dinner (7:00 pm - 11:00 pm).
Price Range: €21 - €40
Closest Subway: Jacques Bonsergent
Address: 116 Avenue Ledru Rollin, 75011 Paris

5. Le Chateaubriand

Basque chef Inaki Aizpitarte will take you on an adventurous food tour here at Le Chateubriand. When he first bought the place, he kept the name of the restaurant and most of the 1930s look, but he added his own unique flair to it. Expect to try combinations you would have never dreamed of putting together, like foie gras served in miso soup, or shucked oysters over pureed acai. Book in advance, as this spot tends to fill up quickly.

Hours: Monday - Sunday for lunch (12:00 pm - 3:00 pm) and dinner (7:00 pm - 11:00 pm).
Price Range: €21 - €40
Closest Subway: Jacques Bonsergent, Goncourt
Address: 29 Avenue Parmentier, 75011 Paris

6. Bistrot Paul Bert

For those who are sincere in their desire to taste classic bistro fare, this is an excellent choice. Inspired by cool local flea market finds, the eclectic interior includes a bright mosaic floor, oversized mirrors, small wooden tables, and interesting chandeliers. The chalkboard menu changes seasonally, but favorites like steak frites are never taken off the menu. Because the portions are generous, the prices are affordable, and there is a whiff of authenticity still hanging in the air. Reservations are a must.
Hours: Tuesday - Saturday for lunch (12:00 pm - 2:00 pm) and dinner (7:30 pm - 11:00 pm). Closed Sunday and Monday.
Price Range: €21 - €40
Closest Subway: Faidherbe-Chaligny (8)
Address: 18 Rue Paul Bert, 75011 Paris

7. Le Chardenoux

Established by the Chardenoux family at the beginning of the 20th century, the namesake restaurant's classical beginnings resonate today with walls of mirrors and engraved glass, beautiful Belle Époque ceiling moulding, and a vast tank of a zinc-topped bar just inside the front door. This is a perfect example of how quintessential French cuisine and vintage decor go hand in hand. Excellent service and an interesting wine list add to the pleasure of a meal at a restaurant that is a long-time Parisian favorite.

Hours: Monday - Sunday for lunch (12:00 pm - 3:00 pm) and dinner (7:00 pm - 11:00 pm).
Price Range: €21 - €40
Closest Subway: Jacques Bonsergent
Address: 1 Rue Jules Vallès, 75011 Paris

8. Le Sixieme Sens

When in the mood for some unpretentious and understated honest-to-goodness French cooking, check out this restaurant. You will be surprised that this cozy place is a one-man-show (the chef, owner, and host are all one person). The food itself is innovative and a must-try. But remember to book in advance, as the place is very small.

Hours: Tuesday - Saturday (7:00 pm - 11:00 pm).
Price Range: €21 - €40
Closest Subway: Bréguet - Sabin
Address: 43, rue de la Roquette, Bastille, 75011 Paris

9. Le Dauphin

This tapas and wine bar is owned by Basque chef Inaki Aizpitarte and is the baby sister of Le Chateaubriand next door. Le Dauphin is a cool and compact joint with a U-shaped central bar, as well as floors and walls decorated in Carrara marble. It is currently one of the trendiest places in the 11th Arrondissement and is an excellent place to enjoy original wine. It has a regularly changing small-plates menu that offers its guest an example of Aizpitarte's adventurous cooking.

Hours: Monday - Sunday for lunch (12:00 pm - 3:00 pm) and dinner (7:00 pm - 11:00 pm).
Price Range: €21 - €40
Closest Subway: Jacques Bonsergent
Address: 131 Avenue Parmentier, 75011 Paris

10. Septime

Septime often appears in every "Must-Eat Places in Paris" list, and for good reason. Remember to try booking in advance because this place is packed to the brim, especially after it got its Michelin star. It is one of the hardest restaurants to get into, but once you are able to book a table, an adventure awaits you. Its young chef Bertrand Grébaut mesmerizes guests with surprisingly inventive dishes while its chic, modern look is both trendy and laidback.

Hours: Monday - Friday (7:30 pm - 10:00 pm), Tuesday - Friday (12:15 pm - 2:00 pm).
Price Range: €30 - €65
Closest Subway: Charonne
Address: 80 Rue de Charonne, 75011 Paris

10 Best Restaurants for 12th Arrondissement:

Near the Gare de Lyon, the 12th Arrondissement is different from the rest of Paris, as it is less touristy and crowded. It is, however, safe and quiet. A must-do in the 12ᵗʰ district is to try some of the many Italian restaurants.

1. Assaporare

Assaporare means *savor* in Italian, and this place offers some incredibly savory Italian dishes! The restaurant was originally owned by an architect, and the interior design is rather meticulous and minimal, but guests come here for the food. With an authentic, honest approach to Italian cuisine and a good-spirited staff, this place is a must-visit!

Hours: Monday - Tuesday (12:00 pm - 2:30 pm), Wednesday - Friday (12:00 pm - 2:30 pm, 7:30 pm - 10:00 pm), and Saturday (7:30 pm - 10:00 pm). Closed Sunday.
Price Range: €21 - €40
Closest Subway: Ledru-Rollin
Address: 7 Rue Saint-Nicolas, 75012 Paris

2. L'Aubergeade

The L'Aubergeade is a family restaurant that serves traditional and modern French dishes. A cozy, laid back ambience and good food await you at a reasonable price.

Hours: Tuesday - Friday (12:00 pm - 2:00 pm) and Saturday - Sunday (12:00 pm - 3:00 pm).
Price Range: €16 - €35
Closest Subway: Ledru-Rollin
Address: 20 Rue d'Aligre, 75012 Paris

3. Miel et Paprika

At this little old nouvelle cuisine bistro, you will have a delicious meal served with flair and attention to detail. Also, as the name of the restaurant suggests, the chef likes to explore dishes with slightly spicy and sweet flavors, which always seem to work together. For example, try the zucchini cake -- it is a sure winner. This little restaurant, with a small menu, creative dishes, and affordable prices, is sure to delight you.

Hours: Tuesday - Friday (7:30 pm - 11:30 pm), Saturday (12:30 pm - 3:00 pm, 7:30 pm - 11:30 pm). Closed Sunday.
Price Range: €21 - €40
Closest Subway: Ledru-Rollin
Address: 24 Rue de Cotte, 75012 Paris

4. Le Picotin

Tucked in a not-so-touristy neighborhood is Le Picotin, a bistro that serves traditional French cuisine with a lovely twist. Picotin was the name of the donkey in a popular comic book, so you will find copies of it inside the restaurant. The food is quite delectable and reasonably priced, and the service is very welcoming. It is no wonder that this bistro has been getting awesome press!

Hours: Monday - Saturday (12:00 pm - 2:30 pm, 7:30 pm - 10:30 pm). Closed Sundays.
Price Range: €11 - €20
Closest Subway: Picpus
Address: 35 rue Sibuet 75012 Paris

5. Sardegna a Tavola

For a true taste of Sardinia in Paris, head to the outreaches of the 12th Arrondissement and you will find this gem. It is easy to be charmed by the room's mellow yellow walls, the colorful graffiti, dried herbs and hams hanging from the ceiling, nautical frescoes, black and white photographs, and shelves of local produce. But the real treat lies in its large Sardinian meals, with enormous richness and variety from one island. You will not be disappointed.

Hours: Monday (7:30 pm - 11:00 pm), Tuesday - Saturday (12:00 pm - 2:30 pm, 7:30 pm - 11:00 pm). Closed Sunday.
Price Range: €21 - €40
Closest Subway: Ledru-Rollin
Address: 1 Rue de Cotte, 75012 Paris

6. A La Biche au Bois

This is a neighborhood bistro that serves generous portions of hearty, traditional dishes from the Southwest of France. With deep bowls of potato puree and piles of frites, or Veal Scaloppini for the main course, you cannot go wrong at A La Biche au Bois! Well-known and loved by Parisians during the game season, the name means "the doe in the forest," so the house special is, of course, la biche. If it is a cold night, this is the perfect spot.

Hours: Monday (7:00 pm - 10:45 pm), Tuesday - Friday (12:00 pm - 2:30 pm, 7:00 pm - 10:45 pm). Closed Saturday and Sunday.
Price Range: €21 - €40
Closest Subway: Gare de Lyon (1, 14, RER A)
Address: 45 Avenue Ledru-Rollin, 75012 Paris

7. Chai 33

Chai 33 is a very large and contemporary restaurant, lounge bar, and wine bar, where wine is the star of the show in every way. Wine lovers are in heaven at Chai 33, since the wine cellar boasts over 300 varieties! The design is avant garde and spectacular, and the two patios boast stunning views of Saint Emilion and Bercy Park. As for cuisine, Chai is popular for its international selections, predominantly its Asian inspired options. With great food, a selection of the best wines, and funky house music, Chai 33 is a wonderful choice -- you cannot go wrong with it!

Hours: Monday - Friday (8:00 am - 2:00 am), Saturday - Sunday (9:00 am - 2:00 am).
Price Range: €21 - €40
Closest Subway: Cour Saint-Émilion
Address: Bercy Village, 33 Cour Saint-Emilion, 75012 Paris

8. Le Pataquès

Conveniently located next to Palais Omnisport de Paris Bercy, Le Pataques is a warm and cheerful French restaurant that brings Provence, and a bit of sunshine, to the streets of Paris in its décor and cuisine. A bright and colorful interior sets the scene for some Mediterranean and Provencal delights, all carefully created by Head Chef Rose Kebir. Kebir offers a very inventive menu full of Provencal dishes and drinks that are hard to find in the French capital. What's more, if it is warm out, you can sit outside on their beautiful terrace!

Hours: Monday - Saturday for lunch (12:00 pm - 2:30 pm) and dinner (7:00 pm - 10:30 pm). Closed Sunday.
Price Range: €20 - €60
Closest Subway: Bercy
Address: 40 Boulevard de Bercy, 75012 Paris

9. Le Tarmac

Le Tarmac is a trendy and contemporary brasserie. The restaurant is modern and bright in style, yet slightly retro with red walls and white tables and chairs. There is a terrace to hang out on when weather permits. Le Tarmac offers its guests not only a fantastic brasserie, but also a well-stocked bar offering cocktails of all kinds and a tapas menu served all day. The menu is varied and dishes mix between east and west, bringing traditional bistro style and exotic flavors together. If you are in town on the weekend, the weekend brunch is extremely popular. If you are looking for great food at very reasonable prices, Le Tarmac is your place.

Hours: Monday - Wednesday (7:30 am - 1:00 am), Thursday - Saturday (7:30 am - 2:00 am). Closed Sunday.
Price Range: €8 - €20
Closest Subway: Gare de Lyon
Address: 33 Rue de Lyon, 75012 Paris

10. Les Provinces

If you find yourself at the Marché d'Aligre, drop by this artisan butcher shop-slash-restaurant for some excellent cuts of meats cooked to order. Pair your rib steak, lamb chops, or pork ribs with some good old sautéed potatoes and a glass of wine, and you are in for a laid back, rocking good time.

Hours: Tuesday - Friday (12:00 pm - 2:00 pm), Saturday - Sunday (12:00 pm - 3:00 pm).
Price Range: €16 - €35
Closest Subway: Ledru-Rollin
Address: 20 Rue d'Aligre, 75012 Paris

10 Best Restaurants for 13th Arrondissement:

The 13th Arrondissement centers on the Place d' Italie and borders the Latin Quarter. Up until the late 1990s, the 13ᵉ Arrondissement was known only for its 1960s tower blocks and exotic Chinatown district. But as the formerly industrial riverside district transformed with a stylish, contemporary makeover, visitors are also rediscovering the many historic buildings and hidden village streets that have escaped modernization. Visitors will notice that the restaurants in this district have also escaped modernization.

1. Au Petit Margue

Au Petit Margue is a pretty little bistro that goes above and beyond customers' expectations. The Cousin brothers, who own and operate this restaurant, are willing to leave the beaten path of bistro fare and offer dishes you typically would not see in a bistro. But fear not -- they also please their faithful public with home-style traditional favorites. The decor is from the 1900s, with red walls and large mirrors, creating a very French feel.

Hours: Monday - Saturday for lunch (12:00 pm - 2:30 pm) and dinner (7:00 pm - 10:00 pm);
 Sunday (7:00 pm - 10:00 pm).
Price Range: €20 - €50
Closest Subway: Gobelins (7)
Address: 9 Boulevard de Port-Royal, 75013 Paris

2. Green Garden

Green Garden is a 100% vegetarian Chinese restaurant. They use only organic produce and no meat, dairy, or GMO food in their cooking. On the menu, you will recognize a wide range of Chinese classics, like stir-fried or braised dishes common to Chinese menus, but they are all made with soy, not meat, and everything is delicious. This is a great spot for vegetarians or for people looking for something new!

Hours: Wednesday - Monday for lunch (12:00 pm - 3:00 pm) and dinner (7:00 pm - 10:00 pm). Closed Tuesday.
Price Range: €8 - €20
Closest Subway: Porte d'Ivry
Address: 20 Rue nationale, 75013 Paris

3. Chez Gladines

This is arguably the best budget-friendly and delicious restaurant in Paris. Chez Gladines is something of a brand name among Parisian bohos and strapped-for-cash students. Inside, a center bar displays the Basque flag and differing sizes of chalkboards with multi-colored descriptions of the night's a la carte items, fixed-price menus, desserts, wines, and beers. This place is nowhere near intimate, so do not expect to go on a romantic date here. The portions are ridiculously large, so come hungry! It is important to note that Chez Gladines does not accept credit cards, so make sure to bring some cash.

Hours: Monday - Sunday for lunch (12:00 pm - 3:00 pm) and dinner (7:00 pm - 1:00 am). Closed Sunday.

Price Range: €8 - €20
Closest Subway: Corvisart
Address: 30 Rue des cinq Diamants, 75013 Paris

4. Il était Un Square

For a quick dinner in a small and cozy place, drop by the Il Etait Un Square. There are a few selections, but if you are craving good burgers with a twist, plus some mouthwatering desserts, this is a cool place to visit.
Hours: Monday - Saturday (8:30 am - 11:00 pm).
Price Range: €11 - €34
Closest Subway: Corvisart
Address: 54 Rue Corvisart, 75013 Paris

5. Le Comptoir du Petit Marguery

Le Comptoir du Petit Marguery is a less expensive option compared to its mother restaurant, Le Petit Margue. It is a small restaurant with factory lamps, brick walls, and wooden tables where guests can enjoy appealing dishes at extremely reasonable prices. It is an excellent address for a low-key, low-budget and very satisfying meal experience.

Hours: Monday - Sunday (12:00 pm - 10:30 pm).
Price Range: €8 - €20
Closest Subway: Les Gobelins
Address: 9 Boulevard de Port-Royal, 75013 Paris

6. L'Ourcine

Inside this gourmet bistro, you will find white walls, white napkins, wood tables and chairs, and a blackboard that lists the current menu of local French specialties from the chef Sylvain Danire. Dishes include options such as fish, seasonal game, and produce. A fixed-price menu with wine pairings is also available, and the dessert menu offers a number of options!
Hours: Tuesday - Saturday for lunch (12:00 pm - 2:30 pm) and dinner (7:00 pm - 10:30 pm). Closed Sunday and Monday.
Price Range: €21 - €40
Closest Subway: Les Gobelins
Address: 92 Rue Broca, 75013 Paris

7. Virgule

Virgule is owned and operated by talented Cambodian chef Dao Heng. This small bistro serves a mixture of classic French cuisine as well as some Asian-French infused dishes for those interested in trying something new. Thanks to its high-quality food and surprisingly low prices, the restaurant has a strong following of locals and tourists alike.

Hours: Thursday - Tuesday for lunch (12:00 pm - 2:30 pm) and dinner (7:30 pm - 11:00 pm). Closed Wednesday.
Price Range: €21 - €40
Closest Subway: Place d'Italie
Address: 9 Rue Véronèse, 75013 Paris

8.   Variations

Previously called L'Olivier, this renovated restaurant located near the Jardin des Plantes offers a diverse menu, from meat to non-meat and fish. Whether you go for the a la carte or the menu du jour, the wide range of dishes are all flavorful and reasonably priced.

Hours: Monday - Friday for lunch (12:00 pm - 3:00 pm) and dinner (7:00 pm - 10:30 pm). Closed Saturday and Sunday.
Price Range: €30 - €60
Closest Subway: Saint-Marcel
Address: 18 rue des Wallons 75013 Paris

9.   L'Auberge du 15

This elegant restaurant has charming, provincial, neo-retro decor, making people feel as if they are in the countryside, not in the middle of Paris. The parquet floors, stone accents, heavy curtains, and blue ceramic tiles on the kitchen walls are reminiscent of chef-owner Nicolas Castelet's family roots in the Aubrac region. Here, he cooks classical French cuisine with a simplified technique and uses seasonal ingredients. Delicately flavored juices and tasty accompaniments can be found in dishes like the asparagus with morels and a "sauté bourguignon" simmered with aromatic vegetables and dry-smoked pig fat, a favorite among the locals.

Hours: Tuesday - Saturday for lunch (12:00 pm - 2:30 pm) and dinner (7:00 pm - 11:00 pm). Closed Sunday and Monday.
Price Range: €20 - €100
Closest Subway: Port Royal (RER B), Saint Jacques (6)
Address: 15 Rue de la Santé, 75013 Paris

10.   L'Avant-Gout

The lovely golden-russet decor creates a calming atmosphere in a place that bustles with people and enthusiasm. L'Avant-Gout is a modern bistro that offers classic French fare. Their menu changes weekly, but the favored dish, port-au-feu, is always on the menu. There is also an impressive wine list and wine cellar where guests can buy bottles to take home with them.
Hours: Tuesday - Saturday for lunch (12:00 pm - 2:00 pm) and dinner (7:30 pm - 11:00 pm). Closed Sunday and Monday.
Price Range: €8 - €20
Closest Subway: Corvisart
Address: 26 Rue Bobillot, 75013 Paris

10 Best Restaurants for 14th Arrondissement:

Although mostly residential, the 14th Arrondissement is best known for the Montparnasse station, the towering skyscraper Tour Montparnasse, the Paris Catacombs, and the Parc Montsouris. The Cité Universitaire is also found in this district and is traditionally known for lively cafés and restaurants around the Boulevard du Montparnasse and the rue Daguerre.

1. Le Dôme

Le Dome is one of this neighborhood's most legendary and historic restaurants. With a completely art deco decor, elegance and tranquility come together in a beautiful, spacious dining room and fully glazed terrace. Le Dome was, and is, renowned as an intellectual gathering place; Paris's artists and politicians have been pushing and shoving to enter this place since it was established in the early 1900s. No matter what you order, you can be assured of its freshness and, therefore, great flavor, but the menu puts a spotlight on fish and seafood.

Hours: Monday - Sunday for lunch (12:00 pm - 3:00 pm) and dinner (7:00 pm - 11:30 pm).
Price Range: €50 - €100
Closest Subway: Vavin (4)
Address: 108 Boulevard du Montparnasse, 75014 Paris

2.   Le Bistrot du Dôme

Le Bistrot du Dome offers great fish at reasonable prices, which brings patrons back again and again. The decor is bright and semi-nautical, and the service is wonderful. Run by the Bras family, who own the Famous Dome Restaurant and the Poissonerie du Dome across the street, this little bistro also offers wine at incredible prices!

Hours: Monday - Sunday for lunch (12:30 pm - 2:00 pm) and dinner (7:30 pm - 11:00 pm).
Price Range: €30 - €50
Closest Subway: Vavin (4)
Address: 1 Rue Delambre, 75014 Paris

3.   La Coupole

Created in 1927, with all the lovely decor of that time, this brasserie, under the same ownership as Brasserie Flo, is also a fixture in the neighborhood. The art deco style is represented by large ceilings with geometric shapes and beautiful floor mosaics. Busy morning through night, expect the usual brasserie fare here. Specialties include the succulent lamb curry and the delicious smoked salmon.

Hours: Monday - Friday (8:30 am - 2:30 pm, 6:30 pm - 12:00 am), and Saturday (8.00am to 8.00pm). Closed Sunday.
Price Range: €21 - €40
Closest Subway: Vavin
Address: 102 Boulevard du Montparnasse, 75014 Paris

4. La Cantine du Troquet

A popular Basque bistro, La Cantine du Troque's specialty is pork. Chef Christian Etchebest lets no part of the pig go to waste: shoulder, ear, chest, fillet cut into slivers with Espelette pepper, the famous black pudding, terrine, slices, gratin, or however else they can dream up. Here, you are definitely in good hands when it comes to pork. There are, of course, other delicious meat options, as well as fish. Be aware that there is no set menu, so come hungry and ready to try whatever Christian decides to prepare that day. There are no reservations, so come early and save some room for dessert, too.

Hours: Tuesday - Saturday (11:45 am - 2:15 pm) and (7:00 pm - 10:45 pm). Closed Sunday and Monday.
Price Range: €20 - €40
Closest Subway: Pernety (13)
Address: 100 Rue de l'Ouest, 75014 Paris

5. Cobéa

If you are looking for something more upscale, drop by Cobéa for a one-of-a-kind gastronomic experience. Located in a wonderfully restored 1920s house, Cobéa will have you experiencing a festival of flavors in your palate, courtesy of its elegant and inventive dishes. You can choose from their pre fixe menu which comes in three choices: four courses, six courses, or eight courses.

Hours: Tuesday - Saturday for lunch and dinner (12:15 pm - 1:15 pm, 7:15 pm - 9:15 pm). Closed Sunday and Monday.
Price Range: €49 - €119
Closest Subway: Gaîté
Address: 11 rue Raymond Losserand 75014 Paris

6. Au Vin des Rues

This Parisian brasserie is a neighborhood favorite, and it is hard to miss with its red facade. Au Vin des Rues serves daily specials and classic bistro dishes like duck breast, andouillett, and steak tartare. They also have a great selection of wines that include options from the Lyonnais and Loire Valley vineyards. And with options like tarte aux framboises and crème brûlée, saving room for dessert at Au Vin des Rues is a must!

Hours: Monday - Saturday for lunch (12:00 pm - 3:00 pm) and dinner (7:30 pm - 10:30 pm). Closed Sunday.
Price Range: €21 - €40
Closest Subway: Denfert-Rochereau
Address: 21 Rue Boulard, 75014 Paris

7. Le Duc

Le Duc isn't the fancy or retro type Parisian restaurant you hear about often, but it has a faithful, laid-back clientele who prefer good quality produce over trends. Le Duc is a seafood restaurant with a blue and white façade and a wood-paneled dining room with fish drawings on the walls that make you feel like you are on a yacht. On the menu is nothing but ultra-fresh fish and seafood, simply prepared to preserve their flavor, like langoustines with ginger and fennel gratin, tartare of sea bass and salmon, grilled sea bream, and Provencal fricassee of monkfish. If you love fish and seafood, why not try Le Duc?

Hours: Tuesday - Friday (12:00 am - 2:00 pm, 8:00 pm - 10:30 pm), and Saturday (8:00 pm - 10:30 pm). Closed Sunday and Monday.
Price Range: €40 - €100
Closest Subway: Raspail
Address: 243 Boulevard Raspail, 75014 Paris

8. Les Fondus De La Raclette

Lovers of cheese will love this great Parisian restaurant! Fondue is the name of the game and boy is it amazing! The interior is warm and inviting, with lots of light wood, neutral colors and a lovely rustic feel. The tables all have their own grill built into them, a nice touch and an important one to keep the quality of the food top class. The menu features a good selection of fondues, raclettes, and grills, and the tastes are truly exquisite. There are also a number of salads to choose from to form the perfect accompaniment. Desserts are also great and reasonably priced. So, if you love cheese, do not miss this one.

Hours: Monday - Sunday (12:30 pm - 2:30 pm) and (7:00 pm - 11:30 pm).
Price Range: €21 - €40
Closest Subway: Vavin
Address: 209 Boulevard Raspail, 75014 Paris

9. Pavillon Montsouris

Pavillon Montsouris is a beautiful belle époque style French restaurant in a quaint historical building. The menu sticks to typical French classic cuisine at reasonable prices. Pavillon Montsouris is particularly popular among business locals during weekdays, and on weekends, it is a hotspot for many Parisians looking for a special treat at a decent price.
Hours: Monday - Saturday for lunch (12:30 pm - 2:30 pm) and dinner (7:30 pm - 10:30 pm); Sunday (12:30 pm - 2:30 pm).
Price Range: €40 - €100
Closest Subway: RER B - Cité Universitaire

Address: 20 Rue Gazan, 75014 Paris

10. Bistrotters

For a casual and laidback dining experience, you can head over to Bistrotters. This much-hailed bistro offers sensational dishes, but it is recommended that you book around 12 days in advance. The long queue, however, is worth it.

Hours: Tuesday - Saturday (12:00 pm - 2:00 pm, 7:00 pm - 10:00 pm).
Price Range: €21 - €40
Closest Subway: Plaisance
Address: 9 rue Decrès 75014 Paris

10 Best Restaurants for 15th Arrondissement:

The 15ᵗʰ Arrondissement is the largest Arrondissement of central Paris. It is a quiet and upscale neighborhood, and is also home to some of the most authentic restaurants and brasseries in all of Paris. This Arrondissement is where you will most likely experience a true taste of Parisian lifestyle.

1. Benkay

Located atop the Novotel Hotel, this is the Japanese restaurant with perhaps the best view, overlooking the Seine river. In a refined and comfortable atmosphere, two of Japan's top sushi chefs offer traditional dishes of sushi, sashimi, tempura, yakitori, grilled meats, and fritters. The Teppan-Yaki is a spectacular cuisine on a hot platter, which is a big hit.

Hours: Monday - Sunday for lunch (12:00 pm - 2:30 pm) and dinner (7:00 pm - 10:30 pm).
Price Range: €40 - €100
Closest Subway: Charles Michels
Address: 61 Quai de Grenelle, 75015 Paris

2. L'Epopée

L'Epopée restaurant offers high-end modern French cuisine. Inside, you will see formally laid tables dressed in white with fresh posies on each table. Serving both traditional and creative French cuisine, the seasonal cooking plays on simple colors, tastes, smells, and textures to form sublime dishes that are almost too elegant to touch or eat. Wine lovers will enjoy the 100+ selections of fine wine from small growers around the area.

Hours: Monday - Sunday for lunch (12:00 pm - 2:00 pm) and dinner (7:30 pm - 10:00 pm).
Price Range: €21 - €40
Closest Subway: Charles Michels
Address: 89 Avenue Emile Zola, 75015 Paris

3. La Dînée

Despite being a bit off the beaten path, La Dînée is a beautiful little restaurant where Chef Christolphe Chabanal offers his wonderfully creative style of cooking.

Hours: Monday - Sunday for lunch (12:30 pm - 2:30 pm) and dinner (7:30 pm - 10:30 pm).
Price Range: €21 - €50
Closest Subway: Balard
Address: 85 Rue Leblanc, 75015 Paris

4. Erawan

Erawan is a small, elegant restaurant with two small dining rooms inside. The minimalist decor at Erawan evokes the mysterious ambience of Southeast Asia, which matches the food. Enjoy generous portions of authentic Thai cuisine that is full of flavor. A specialty worth trying is the shrimp steamed in banana leaves. For vegetarians struggling in Paris, you will be delighted to find delicious tofu versions of most dishes!

Hours: Monday (7:00 pm - 10:30 pm), Tuesday - Saturday (12:00 pm - 10:30 pm). Closed Sunday.
Price Range: €21 - €40
Closest Subway: Dupleix
Address: 76 Rue de la Fédération, 75015 Paris

5. Jadis

Young chef Guillaume Delage serves a gently updated take on classic French cuisine (Jadis means "in days gone by") and guests are guaranteed an authentic and intimate dining experience. The naturally lit interior consists of black tables and gray hues, highlighted by plum accents and colorful pieces of art. The blackboard menu is limited in its selection and changes regularly. Do not miss the amazing cheese trolley or the deconstructed desserts after your main course!

Hours: Monday - Friday for lunch (12:00 pm - 2:00 pm) and dinner (7:00 pm - 11:00 pm). Closed Saturday and Sunday.
Price Range: €20 - €50
Closest Subway: Convention (12)
Address: 208 Rue de la Croix Nivert, 75015 Paris

6. Café du Commerce

When it opened in 1921, this three-level restaurant with a central atrium full of plants and some art deco interior was a bouillon, or a place people went for a fast, cheap meal. With the arrival of new owners Marie and Etienne Gerraud in 2003, the quality has soared but prices remain reasonable, and they now serve excellent oysters, onion soup, œufs mayonnaise, and superb Limousin beef. Try their frites, too!

Hours: Monday - Sunday for lunch (12:00 pm - 3:00 pm) and dinner (7:00 pm - 12:00 am).
Price Range: €21 - €40
Closest Subway: Avenue Émile Zola
Address: 51 Rue du Commerce, 75015 Paris

7. L'Epicuriste

Due to incredible success and not enough room in L'Epigramme in the Saint Germain region, Stéphane Marcuzzi and Chef Aymeric Kraml opened L'Epicuriste because they needed more room! L'Epicuriste is much more spacious, if a bit noisy, and Kraml's cooking is as good as ever. The prices may have gone up since their move, but the quality and creativity of the kitchen remain outstanding.
Hours: Tuesday - Saturday for lunch (12:00 pm - 2:00 pm) and dinner (7:00 pm - 10:00 pm). Closed Sunday and Monday.
Price Range: €20 - €50
Closest Subway: Pasteur (6, 12)
Address: 41 Boulevard Pasteur, 75015 Paris

8.   142 Crêperie Contemporaine

Inside this small creperie, you will find plush brown chairs, polished wooden tables, and beautiful lanterns. In addition to the traditional sweet crepes offered - like banana and chocolate - the affordable menu also includes savory Normandy-style galettes -- thin, square pancakes made with dark buckwheat flour. Fillings range from ham, egg, and cheese to more unusual options like blood sausage with apples and potatoes. No wonder this is one of President Nicolas Sarkozy's favorite restaurants! There is also a terrace, which is enclosed and warmed with heat lamps during the winter.

Hours: Monday - Saturday for lunch (12:00 pm - 2:30 pm) and dinner (7:00 pm - 10:30 pm). Closed Sunday.
Price Range: €8 - €20
Closest Subway: Charles Michels
Address: 59 Rue Saint-Charles, 75015 Paris

9.   Restaurant du Marché

Restaurant du Marche ⬜is a French bistro that offers a varied menu, inspired by a provincial setting. Favorites include duck breast with honey and rabbit with rosemary. They also have dishes that change daily to keep up with fresh produce. There is a terrace available which is perfect when weather permits, but is also heated in the winter.

Hours: Tuesday - Saturday for lunch (12:00 pm - 2:00 pm) and dinner (7:30 pm - 10:00 pm). Closed Sunday and Monday.
Price Range: €8 - €20
Closest Subway: Porte de Versailles
Address: 59 Rue de Dantzig, 75015 Paris

10. Le Grand Pan

Benoit Gauthier's fantastic neighborhood bistro is a must for carnivores looking to sit down with a group of friends around a rustic farmhouse table to get their fill of enormous cuts of grilled meat, washed down with delicious French (natural) wines. At dinner, a complimentary starter of soup is served, and then you choose your meat of choice, many of which are designed for two people. Everything comes with a delicious mountain of homemade fries and a green salad. Do not forget to try their amazing desserts!

Hours: Monday - Friday for lunch (12:00 pm - 2:00 pm) and dinner (7:30 pm - 11:00 pm). Closed Saturday and Sunday.
Price Range: €20 - €50
Closest Subway: Convention (12)
Address: 20 Rue Rosenwald, 75015 Paris

10 Best Restaurants for 16th Arrondissement:

The 16th Arrondissement is located on the West Side of Paris and hosts a large number of embassies, as well as the wealthy residential districts of Auteuil and Passy. The 16th has a calm town vibe rather than a city feel to it. The 16th Arrondissement is widely considered to be the neighborhood of Paris' wealthy; however, while many restaurants confirm this, there are still some that are very reasonably priced.

1. Jamin

Classic, traditional and formal, Jamin is a bit of a quiet Parisian institution, having helped shape the careers of the likes of Joel Robuchon, who earned his third Michelin star here. The space has been updated and revamped with mod accents of ethnic art, taupe walls, and dark wood floors. The menu features both old school French recipes, such as the Paris Brest (crown of choux pastry filled with whipped cream and sprinkled with almonds), as well as Asian style dishes with a Gallic twist (sea bass in a creamy coconut-curry sauce).

Hours: Monday - Sunday for lunch (12:00 pm - 2:30 pm) and dinner (7:00 pm - 10:30 pm). Closed Saturday and Sunday.
Price Range: €21 - €40
Closest Subway: Boissière
Address: 32 Rue de Longchamp, 75116 Paris

2. Le Stella

If you want to try something hailed by the locals as a "true brasserie", Le Stella is a nice place to check out. Serving traditional French fare at an efficient speed, the place is mostly packed with a mix of locals and some tourists who want to sample its amazing seafood dishes.

Hours: Monday - Friday for lunch (12:00 pm - 3:30 pm) and dinner (7:00 pm - 12:00 am).
Price Range: €21 - €40
Closest Subway: Rue de la Pompe
Address: 133 Ave. Victor Hugo, 75016 Paris

3. Chez Geraud

Although Chef Geraud Roniger used to run this place, there was a change of ownership for this chic and cozy bistro. Regardless, you are still promised a warm welcome, excellent traditional cuisine made with the freshest ingredients in a charming dining room, and great prices! □

Hours: Monday - Friday for lunch (12:00 pm - 2:00 pm) and dinner (7:30 pm - 10:00 pm); Saturday (7:30 pm - 10:00 pm). Closed Sunday.
Price Range: €40 - €100
Closest Subway: La Muette (9)
Address: 31 Rue Vital, 75016 Paris

4. Le Pré Catelan

Owned by the famous Pastry Chef Lenotre since 1976, Le Pre Catelan is located in a magnificent 1850s pavilion set in the heart of the expansive Bois de Boulogne Park. This restaurant has 3 Michelin stars and serves amazing cuisine that is both subtle and generous. During the warmer months, seating is also available outside beneath the chestnut trees.
Hours: Tuesday - Saturday for lunch (12:00 pm - 2:00 pm) and dinner (7:30 pm - 10:30 pm). Closed Sunday and Monday.

Price Range: €130 - €280
Closest Subway: Saint-Lazare
Address: Route de Suresnes, 75016 Paris Bois de Boulogne

5. Monsieur Bleu

Located inside the Palais de Tokyo, Monsieur Bleu certainly enjoys a superb setting with its Art Deco dining room in grey, green and gold decor, and its terrace looking out onto the Seine and Eiffel Tower. Designed by French architect Joseph Dirand, the interior cleverly combines classical and contemporary with a cool, minimalist feel. The restaurant is named after a fictional character, and it goes against the color palette of blues that one might expect. The dishes, sophisticated and full of flavor, are not to be outdone. Come here to see and be seen!

Hours: Monday - Sunday (12:00 pm - 12:00 am).
Price Range: €21 - €40
Closest Subway: léna
Address: 20 Avenue de New York, 75116 Paris

6. Cristal Room Baccarat

In the middle of the first floor of the Maison Baccarat, the Cristal Room restaurant offers an inventive cuisine, made up by the Michelin-starred chef, Guy Martin. Designer Philippe Starck has restored the 18th-century elegance of Maison Baccarat in the Cristal Room Baccarat restaurant, which used to be a private hotel of Marie-Laure de Noailles, with gilded mirrors, Baccarat crystal candles, chandeliers, and brick set in wood paneling.
Hours: Monday - Saturday for lunch (12:30 pm - 2:30 pm) and dinner (7:30 pm - 10:30 pm). Closed Sunday.
Price Range: €36 - €600
Closest Subway: Boissière
Address: 11 Place des États-Unis, 75116 Paris

7. Les Tablettes

Having been trained by Alain Ducasse for many years, Chef Jean-Louis Nomicos decided to open up his own restaurant. In Les Tablettes, Nomicos expresses himself with foods which are heavily influenced by Mediterranean style. Since Nomicos is from Marseille, a city by the Mediterranean sea, menu items definitely have a strong influence in Nomicos background. The excellent menu is enhanced with a homey and sincere environment. The interior of Les Tablettes is sophisticatedly handled to create a comfortable ambience for diners to enjoy their dining experience with their families or friends.

Hours: Monday - Sunday for lunch (12:00 pm - 2:30 pm) and dinner (7:00 pm - 10:30 pm).
Price Range: €40 - €200
Closest Subway: Victor Hugo (2)
Address: 16 Avenue Bugeaud, 75116 Paris

8. L'Abeille

Inside Shangri-La Hotel, chef Philippe Labbé (awarded "Chef of the year 2013" by Gault & Millau) serves refined French fine dining using produce of exceptional quality, enhanced by the presentation of the dishes. Not only will the dishes satisfy your taste buds, but they are also very visually appealing. At this French 2 Michelin-starred fine dining restaurant, attention has been paid to the minutest details of the decor, stylish and minimal, and to the unique and fabulous tableware.

Hours: Tuesday - Saturday (7:00 am - 10:30 pm). Closed Sunday and Monday.
Price Range: €88 - €250
Closest Subway: Iéna (9)
Address: 10 avenue d'Iena | Shangri-La Hotel, Paris - Lobby Level, 75116 Paris, France

9. L'Ogre

In this new classy French bistro owned by a trio who used to own a wine boutique for years, you will be dazzled not only by the spectacular food but also by the fantastic views of the Eiffel Tower. L'Ogre serves some of the best homey classic French bistro cooking that is devoured with pleasure by its guests. The wine selection is great, with many wines you will not find in many establishments. For smokers, L'Ogre also features a great humidor where you do not have to go outside to have a cigarette. The price is very affordable, with most dishes around 16/20 Euros, all the while maintaining outstanding quality.

Hours: Monday - Friday for lunch (12:00 pm - 2:30 pm) and dinner (8:00 pm - 2:00 am). Closed Saturday and Sunday.
Price Range: €30 - €60
Closest Subway: Javel - André Citroën
Address: 1 Avenue de Versailles, 75016 Paris

10. L'Astrance

L'Astrance is a Paris hot spot, having been opened in 2000 by chef Pascal Barbot. There is no a la carte menu here, only a lunch menu and a seasonal dinner menu. Barbot's cooking at this tiny restaurant borders on fusion, with spices used in place of salt in some instances and minimal use of cream and butter. Representative dishes include grilled lamb with miso-lacquered eggplant, sautéed pigeon, and turbot flavored with lemon and ginger. The chef's contemporary cooking style is mirrored by an equally modern dining room with twenty-five buttery yellow leather seats on the ground floor and a dozen more on the open mezzanine. Book in advance!

Hours: Tuesday - Friday for lunch (12:00 pm - 3:30 pm) and dinner (7:00 pm - 10:30 pm). Closed Saturday, Sunday and Monday.
Price Range: €70 - €210
Closest Subway: Passy (6)
Address: 4 Rue Beethoven, 75016 Paris

10 Best Restaurants for 17th Arrondissement:

The 17th Arrondissement is not a typical tourist area, but it is in close proximity to the 8th Arrondissement and, therefore, close to the Champs Elysees and the grand department stores of that lovely area. The southern part of the seventeenth is a trendy area with good restaurants and bars, and its large boulevards and traditional architecture give it a very elegant feel.

1. Le Boeuf Volant

At Le Beouf Volant, the beef here is simply stunning. Chef Jonathan Capitaine has traveled the meat world to get his supply of Australian, Bavarian, American, and Spanish meats. This chic little steakhouse with a small, open kitchen, a dining room with hanging lamps, vintage crockery and plain wooden furniture reminds you of a New York-style steakhouse. A dimly lit and welcoming place, the cozy atmosphere is emphasized by the minimal number of seats.

Hours: Tuesday - Saturday (7:00 pm - 11:00 pm). Closed Sunday and Monday.
Price Range: €21 - €40
Closest Subway: Rome ou Place de Clichy
Address: 4 Rue Mariotte, 75017 Paris

2. Roca

With rough stonewalls, hardwood floors, a counter, and bar stools, this beautiful neo-bistro is definitely a hot spot and worth all the hype. Although the menu is fairly short with four options for each starter, main course, and dessert, it varies widely in ingredients and flavors. The dishes are sometimes surprising and always full of flavor, the cooking is simple, creative and elegant, and the dishes are executed with real charm.

Hours: Monday - Friday for lunch (12:00 pm - 3:00 pm) and dinner (7:30 pm - 1:00 am). Closed Saturday and Sunday.
Price Range: €10 - €40
Closest Subway: Porte de Champerret (3), Pereire (3)
Address: 31, rue Guillaume Tell, 75017 Paris, France

3. La Braisière Jacques Faussat

Be prepared to be impressed at La Braisière. Chef Jacques Faussat has earned one Michelin star at this charming little restaurant that serves wonderful French cuisine in a cozy setting. La Brasserie feels somehow like the dining room in a private home; with thick carpeting, fabric on the walls, and enough elbow room, it all contributes to an intimate dining experience. This French gastronomic cuisine changes with the seasons, and it has a revisited, traditional repertoire, much inspired by Faussat's rooms in the Gers region of France. ☐Faussat enjoys serving simple, tasty, inventive food in a contemporary, cozy setting. There is also a great wine list.

Hours: Monday - Friday for lunch (12:00 pm - 2:30 pm) and dinner (7:30 pm - 10:30 am); Saturday (7:30 pm - 10:30 pm). Closed Sunday.
Price Range: €8 - €20
Closest Subway: Wagram

Address: 54 Rue Cardinet, 75017 Paris

4. Café d'Angel

After spending several years in restaurants like Alain Reix and Le Jules Verne, Jean-Marc decided to open up his own restaurant with wife Mirielle to share his cuisine and experience, all while adding an Alsatian and Perigourdine touch to his creations. Cafe d'Angel is a trendy little bistro with great food and reasonable prices. Try the burger and the creme brulee au chocolat for dessert -- you will not be disappointed!

Hours: Tuesday - Sunday for lunch (11:00 am - 2:00 pm) and dinner (6:00 pm - 10:00 pm). Closed Monday.
Price Range: €21 - €40
Closest Subway: Ternes
Address: 16 Rue Brey, 75017 Paris

5. Chez Gabrielle

For an elegant dinner, Chez Gabrielle is a nice option. With great food and a location quietly tucked away off the beaten path, this place will not make a big dent in your budget.

Hours: Monday - Friday for lunch (12:00 pm - 2:00 pm) and Monday - Saturday for dinner (7:00 pm - 10:00 pm).
Price Range: €21 - €40
Closest Subway: Ternes
Address: 7 Rue Etoile, 75017 Paris

6. Rech

The seafood brasserie Rech has been around since 1925, but it did not turn into one of the best fish houses in Paris until Alain Ducasse took over several years ago. The menu evolves according to the seasons and the catch of the day, but favorites like fruits de mer and oyster platters have kept their place on the menu. Non-seafood eaters are catered to as well, with dishes such as a fricassee of chicken, crayfish, or steak. Rech is an excellent choice for a suave and very Parisian meal.

Hours: Tuesday - Saturday for lunch (12:00 pm - 2:00 pm) and dinner (7:30 pm - 10:00 pm). Closed Sunday and Monday.
Price Range: €40 - €150
Closest Subway: Ternes (2)
Address: 62 Avenue des Ternes, 75017 Paris

7. Dessirier

One of Paris' favorite fish restaurants, Dessirier was an oyster-house for more than a century when Michel Rostang took over to create a sort of fish-brasserie and wet-fish stall, but bursting with chic style. The aqua awning lets you know you have arrived, as does the wood paneling and button-upholstered leather banquets inside. Dishes are centered on fruits de mer, with menu items that include starters of classic fish soup with aioli, main dishes that depend on the catch, like roast turbot and poached or roasted lobsters, as well as land dishes like wild duck with wood mushrooms. There is also a large and affordable wine list to delight wine lovers!

Hours: Monday - Sunday for lunch (12:00 pm - 1:30 pm) and dinner (7:00 pm - 10:00 pm).
Price Range: €40 - €100
Closest Subway: Pereire
Address: 9 Place du Maréchal Juin, 75017 Paris

8. Frédéric Simonin

His contemporary French cooking is light, politely inventive, and full of flavor. This restaurant is pricey, but if you go for lunch, there is a 38 Euro lunch menu option. The setting, the service, and, most of all, the superb cooking, warrant the hefty tabs.

Hours: Tuesday - Saturday for lunch (12:00 pm - 2:30 pm) and dinner (7:30 pm - 10:45 pm). Closed Sunday and Monday.
Price Range: €40 - €100
Closest Subway: Ternes (2)
Address: 25 Rue Bayen, 75017 Paris

9. L'Entredgeu

L'Entredgeu is a place adored by locals. The name comes from noted chef-owner Phillipe Tredgeu, who manages the cooking, and his wife, who expertly runs the front of the house. The tiny, unpretentious restaurant is typically crammed, and the snug arrangement of the tables makes casual chatter with neighboring diners almost unavoidable. Waiters carry a blackboard menu announcing the seasonal bistro fare, which can include battered oysters, caramelized pork belly, and quail with foie gras. The fixed-price menu presents a real bargain, around 30 Euros for classic, well-prepared French cuisine.

Hours: Tuesday - Saturday for lunch (12:00 pm - 2:00 pm) and dinner (7:30 pm - 10:40 pm). Closed Sunday and Monday.
Price Range: €21 - €40
Closest Subway: Porte de Champerret (3)
Address: 83 Rue Laugier, 75017 Paris

10. Agapé

Agapé is a fabulous Michelin-starred restaurant that serves French cuisine. A smart and contemporary setting designed by Andree Putman and including Bernardaud porcelain and Starcke light installations provides the backdrop for some truly exquisite plates of food. As far as cuisine goes, natural and fresh produce of the season are the stars here at Agape. Flavored dishes are crispy, well garnished, and express elegance and subtlety. Here, guests will have a truly a memorable and exquisite dining experience.

Hours: Monday - Friday for lunch (12:00 pm - 2:30 pm) and dinner (8:00 pm - 10:30 pm). Closed Saturday and Sunday.
Price Range: €40 - €100
Closest Subway: Wagram

Address: 51 Rue Jouffroy d'Abbans, 75017 Paris

10 Best Restaurants for 18th Arrondissement:

The 18ᵗʰ Arrondissement of Paris is on the right bank of the Seine. The 18ᵗʰ is home to some of Paris's best loved sights, from the red light district of Pigalle, the artists of Montmartre, to the famous flea markets of Clignancourt. Full of fantastic restaurants and home to the Bohemian café society of Montmartre, soak up the atmosphere and enjoy the food in this truly unique part of Paris.

1. Miroir

This friendly modern bistro's interior is decorated with big framed mirrors (hence the name). Red banquettes and a glass ceiling in the back give it character, while the very professional food and service reflect the owners' haute cuisine training. A slate-board menu brings the focus to the fresh, seasonal food, such as grilled fish or duck breast with chanterelles. An affordable lunch option, the prix fixe menu, includes an entree, the ideal wine accompaniment, and a gourmet cafe.
Hours: Tuesday - Saturday for lunch (12:00 pm - 2:30 pm) and dinner (7:00 pm - 11:00 pm); Sunday (12:00 pm - 2:30 pm). Closed Monday.
Price Range: €20 - €50
Closest Subway: Abbesses (12)
Address: 94 Rue des Martyrs, 75018 Paris

2. La Table d'Eugène

Although La Table d'Eugène is located in the far northern reaches of the 18th Arrondissement, an area that neither many tourists nor many a Parisian normally gets to, all of us would declare the bistro absolutely worth the trek. It is declared to be one of the best restaurants in Montmartre with incredibly affordable prices. The bistro, run by a husband-and-wife team, has a family atmosphere, with the husband in the back and the wife up front -- she is very friendly, almost grandmotherly, but very professional. They cook up some magnificent food using simple flavors, all skillfully assembled and beautifully presented. If you are on a budget, try La Table d'Eugene!

Hours: Tuesday - Saturday for lunch (12:00 pm - 2:00 pm) and dinner (7:30 pm - 10:00 pm). Closed Sunday and Monday.
Price Range: €20 - €40
Closest Subway: Marcadet-Poissonniers (4, 12)
Address: 18 Rue Eugène Sue, 75018 Paris

3. Le Coq Rico

Le Coq Rico welcomes its guests with all the warmth and snugness of a mountain chalet. At this chic and discreet place created by the famous Strasbourg chef Antoine Westermann, as the restaurant name states, chicken is the name of the game. Find Challans free-range chicken, Touraine géline chicken, Bresse poultry, and several other options all artfully roasted and smelling succulent. Those who love poultry will not be disappointed.
Hours: Monday - Sunday (12:00 pm - 12:00 am).
Price Range: €20 - €40

Closest Subway: Blanche (2), Abbesses (12)
Address: 98 Rue Lepic, 75018 Paris

4.   Au Clocher de Montmartre

Owner and Chef of several restaurants in the area, Antoine Heerah has taken it upon himself to reinvent the food scene in Montmartre. The Clocher de Montmartre is no exception; it serves an inventive yet satisfying cuisine in a modern dining room. The smartly decorated spot extends customary Paris dining hours and is open daily, serving nonstop from noon to 10:30 pm. The kitchen offers a mix-and-match of a varied selection of snacks, as well as more elaborated dishes like braised pork with a lemon confit sauce.

Hours: Tuesday - Sunday for lunch (12:00 pm - 3:00 pm) and dinner (7:00 pm - 11:00 pm). Closed Monday.
Price Range: €10 - €40
Closest Subway: Lamarck-Caulaincourt (12)
Address: 10 Rue Lamarck, 75018 Paris

5.   La Mascotte

Founded in 1889, this unassuming bar is about as authentic as it gets in Montmartre. It specializes in quality seafood – oysters, lobster, scallops, and regional dishes as well. The seafood platters are La Mascotte's specialty and the fish is brought in fresh, daily.
Hours: Monday - Sunday (8:00 am - 11:30 pm).
Price Range: €21 - €40
Closest Subway: Abbesses
Address: 52 Rue des Abbesses, 75018 Paris

6.   Seb'on

This is a small restaurant but it is packed with all the best French flavors! This place has only been open for a short time, but the rave reviews are already piling up. Owned by partners Sebastien (the chef) and Dorota (the hostess), this small restaurant located in the heart of Montmartre is being hailed by connoisseurs and regular foodies alike as a new place of awesome gastronomic delights. It is a cozy place with only 11 tables, so make sure to book in advance.

Hours: Wednesday - Saturday for dinner (7:00 pm - 11:00 pm), Saturday and Sunday for lunch (12:00 pm - 3:00 pm).
Price Range: €21 - €40
Closest Subway: Abbesses
Address: 62 rue d'Orsel, 75018 Paris

7.   Chamarré Montmartre

Chef Antoine Heerah, who previously ran the one-star restaurant Chamarré in the 7th Arrondissement, has moved to the former quarters of Beauvilliers, an old-school see-and-be-seen place with an ornate Napoleon III decor. The new dining room has an open kitchen that allows diners to watch as the kitchen team assembles the creative plates. You can also opt to sit on the terrace for a view of the hilly Montmartre neighborhood. Chamarre Montmartre has some of the best seafood in Paris, as well as an incredible-tasting menu concentrating on French and Mauritian fusion food.

Hours: Monday - Sunday for lunch (12:00 pm - 3:00 pm) and dinner (7:00 pm - 11:00 pm).
Price Range: €20 - €100
Closest Subway: Lamarck-Caulaincourt (12)
Address: 52 Rue Lamarck, 75018 Paris

8. Chéri Bibi

Occupying a storefront space with folding doors that open up in good weather, Chéri Bibi is one of the hottest new bistros in Paris. The bar of this restaurant fills up quickly with local artists, musicians, actors, and the Bobos that have taken over the area. The ambiance here is low key, the tables are topped with Kraft paper place mats, and decked out vintage flea market style chairs add to the charm. The food is retro French traditional, including terrine, cote de veau, and steak frites maison, plus a decent selection of wines to help wash it all down. Overall, this is a great place to try if you are into the hip scene!

Hours: Monday - Saturday (6:00 pm - 2:00 am).
Price Range: €21 - €40
Closest Subway: Château Rouge
Address: 15 Rue André del Sarte, 75018 Paris

9. L'Olympic Café

This community bar serves African-influenced specialties for lunch and dinner in the energetic Goutte d'Or district. Housed in a 1930s Art Deco building with the dining area upstairs and the basement downstairs, both are designed with simple furniture and African-style artwork on the wall. This is one of the best places to catch live African music, along with jazz and reggae at night!

Hours: Tuesday - Saturday (5:00 pm - 2:00 am). Closed Sunday and Monday.
Price Range: €2.50 - €13
Closest Subway: Château Rouge
Address: 20 Rue Léon, 75018 Paris

10. Guilo-Guilo

Guilo-Guilo is a Japanese restaurant that serves some spectacular cuisine. The sleek layout, which has seats arranged around an open kitchen, allows diners to watch Chef Eiichi Edakuni and his team chop away at their fish and veggies. It is counter-service only, unless you reserve one of the small banquet rooms; in that case, there is a single six-to-eight delicious dish tasting menu served nightly. Gulio-Gulio is definitely worth a detour if you are a fan of Japanese food with a twist.

Hours: Tuesday - Sunday (7:00 pm - 12:00 am). Closed Monday.
Price Range: €41 - €100
Closest Subway: Abbesses (12)
Address: 8 Rue Garreau, 75018 Paris

10 Best Restaurants for 19th Arrondissement:

Since the recent developments of La Villette and the ornate park of Buttes Chaumont, this part of the city has stirred a lot of interest. La Villette has undergone construction and now offers a canal-side recreation park with its promenades, parks, cinemas, and restaurants. The Les Buttes Chaumont area is mostly a residential neighborhood with many ethnic restaurants and cafes.

1. Le Chapeau Melon

Originally founded as an organic wine shop, Le Chapeau Melon later became a mini restaurant. Oliver Camus, the chef and sommelier of Le Chapeau Melon, has hundreds of bottles lining the walls that come from small and often obscure winemakers. A la carte two nights a week and prix fixe the others, the menu has everything from Japanese-inspired entrées to Italianesque pork carpaccio. Book in advance.

Hours: Wednesday - Sunday (8:30 pm - 11:00 pm). Closed Monday and Tuesday.
Price Range: €20 - €40
Closest Subway: Pyrenées or Belleville (11)
Address: 92 Rue Rebeval, 75019 Paris

2. Pavillon Puebla

Situated in a beautiful building built under Napoleon III, this lovely restaurant is both historic and artistic. There are three dining rooms, all of which are elegant and luxurious. There is also a beautiful terrace. The restaurant is run by a small group of Italians who aim to please, and the food at Pavillon Puebla is focused on Mediterranean cuisine, particularly gourmet Italian. Reservations are strongly recommended.

Hours: Monday - Sunday (8:00 pm - 11:00 pm).
Price Range: €40 - €100
Closest Subway: Buttes Chaumont
Address: Parc des Buttes Chaumont, Avenue Darcel, 75019 Paris

3. Quedubon

The name Restaurant Quedubon (meaning "everything is good") says it all: for those that love traditional French food, this is a perfect address. Quedubon is also an organic wine bar, and owner Gilles Benard introduces his guests to a chalkboard listing of more than 150 wines. Decorated in modern interior like wooden floors, a tasteful gray and red color palette, natural lighting, and a friendly atmosphere, Quedubon is a place to linger and savor an amazing French dish with a great glass of red wine.

Hours: Monday - Saturday for lunch (12:30 pm - 2:30 pm) and dinner (8:00 pm - 10:30 pm), Sunday for lunch only (12:30 pm - 2:30 pm).
Price Range: €20 - €40
Closest Subway: Buttes Chaumont (7bis)
Address: 22 Rue du Plateau, 75019 Paris

4. Au Boeuf Couronné

Meat is king at Au Boeuf Couronné, which truly is a carnivore's paradise. Here, quality meat is served☐by professional traditional waiters who can tell you where each cut of meat comes from, and portions are generous. This spot has a charming, laidback, and old-school feel to it. It is a bit pricey, but not excessive. There is also a fixed-price menu option available.

Hours: Monday - Sunday for lunch (12:00 pm - 3:00 pm) and dinner (7:00 pm - 12:00 am).
Price Range: €21 - €40
Closest Subway: Porte de Pantin (5)
Address: 188 Avenue Jean Jaurès, 75019 Paris

5. Café de la Musique

Café de la Musique has been totally revamped to include a cocktail bar, an open kitchen, another bar, a dining room, and a terrace overlooking historical monuments in the cultural area of Parc de la Villette. The cafe de la Musique has a modern, chic interior with white marble bars, along with lots of wood and stone, and there are different areas where you can sit and relax on sofas and bar stools. You can also opt for a traditional-style dining experience. The fare served is traditional French cuisine.

Hours: Monday - Sunday (9:30 am - 1:00 am).
Price Range: €8 - €30
Closest Subway: Porte de Pantin
Address: 213 avenue Jean-Jaurès, 75019 Paris

6. Chez Arnaud

When in the mood for some excellent burgers and pizza, this neighborhood bistro fits the bill quite nicely. Chez Arnaud is located on a quiet street just near the Philharmonie, so it is ideal to visit before or after watching a concert.
Hours: Tuesday - Sunday for lunch (11:00 am - 3:00 pm) and dinner (7:00 pm - 11:00 pm).
Price Range: €13 - €16
Closest Subway: Porte de Pantin
Address: 16 rue Eugene Jumin, 75019 Paris

7. Hobbes Paris

This one is a new vegan and vegetarian spot that is creating quite the hype. The vegetarian menu changes regularly depending on the seasons, with fresh, bright, and organic dishes to choose from. Mains are priced at around €10 for generous, flavorful servings. Without being revolutionary, Hobbes more than does the job of making you feel cherished and revived without having to splurge on calories or spend all of your euros. This is definitely one of the best vegan and vegetarian restaurants in Paris. Do not forget to try the dessert!

Hours: Tuesday - Wednesday (11:00 am - 4:00 pm); Thursday - Saturday (11:00 am - 4:00 pm) and (7:00 pm - 11:00 pm); Sunday (11:00 am - 4:00 pm). Closed Monday.
Price Range: €8 - €20
Closest Subway: Pyrénées ou Buttes Chaumont

Address: 31 avenue Simon Bolivar, 75019 Paris

8.   Le Laumière

When craving seafood while you are in the area, Le Laumiere is a good place to try. They serve really good bouillabaisse, fish, and enticing desserts, all at a reasonable price.

Hours: Tuesday - Saturday for lunch (12:00 pm to 2:30 pm) and dinner (7:00 pm - 10:00 pm); Sunday for lunch (12:00 pm - 2:30 pm).
Price Range: €21 - €40
Closest Subway: Laumière
Address: 4 rue Petit, 75019 Paris

9.   Le Pacifique

Le Pacifique is a sprawling Cantonese restaurant with amazing food. The old-fashioned decor is not without charm, and the spacious yet intimate neighborhood venue makes you feel at home. It is one of the best spots in Paris for dim sum and crispy skinned pork and duck. Start with a few steamed dishes like dumplings in five flavors or little rice pancakes with prawns. Follow it up with generous, cheap servings of Cantonese rice, or the long-roasted meats. All this, plus beer, is not much more than €20 a person. It is super affordable!

Hours: Monday - Sunday (11:00 am - 2:00 am).
Price Range: €8 - €20
Closest Subway: Belleville
Address: 35 Rue de Belleville, 75019 Paris

10. L'Atlantide

Come for the couscous, stay for the beautiful décor and excellent atmosphere. This little gem has reaped a lot of good reviews, and for good reason. Hailed as having the best couscous in town, L'Atlantide is a good place to visit when you find yourself in the neighborhood.

Hours: Sunday - Thursday (7:00 pm - 10:30 pm), Friday - Saturday (7:00 pm - 11:00 pm), and Saturday - Sunday (12:00 pm - 2:30 pm).
Price Range: €22 - €45
Closest Subway: Laumière
Address: 7 ave Laumière, 75019 Paris

10 Best Restaurants for 20th Arrondissement:

The 20ᵗʰ Arrondissement is east of the city center and represents an old working-class area now in rapid transformation. The main tourist attraction here is the Père-Lachaise Cemetery, where many famous people are buried. For travelers interested in music and culture, this relatively gritty area is great to get to know. There are nightclubs and cafés that specialize in everything from punk-rock to world music, both in the Bagnolet neighborhood south of the cemetery and in the Ménilmontant neighborhood north of the cemetery.

1.   Le Baratin

In this cheerful little bistro and wine bar, Argentine chef Raquen Carena serves homely cooking with an occasional exotic twist. Classics include red tuna tartare with black cherries and foie gras with lentils. Most of the wines at Le Baratin are organic. The street outside Le Baratin is crowded and car-lined, but once inside, a relaxed, family-friendly ambience welcomes you, with decor including artwork on the walls, a mosaic tiled floor, and a chalkboard menu.

Hours: Tuesday - Friday for lunch (12:00 pm - 2:30 pm) and dinner (8:00 pm - 11:30 pm); Saturday (8:00 pm - 11:30 pm). Closed Sunday and Monday.
Price Range: €10 - €60
Closest Subway: Pyrenées or Belleville (11)
Address: 3 Rue Jouye-Rouve, 75020 Paris

2.   Les Allobroges

Casual and elegantly comfortable, Les Allobroges makes you feel like you are dining at home. The food here is classic French and the products of are of great quality, not to mention the homemade bread, which is a great touch. Refined, quality cooking, cozy atmosphere, attentive servers, and affordable prices -- what's not to love?

Hours: Monday - Saturday for lunch (12:00 pm - 2:00 pm) and dinner (7:30 pm - 11:00 pm); Sunday (12:00 pm - 2:30 pm).
Price Range: €21 - €40
Closest Subway: Maraîchers
Address: 71 Rue des Grands Champs, 75020 Paris

3.   Le Jourdain

In the mood for some seafood, tapas, and an authentic French gastropub experience? This is a great place to try. The price is not bad either!

Hours: Tuesday - Saturday (12:00 pm - 11:00 pm). Closed Sunday and Monday.
Price Range: €6 - €24
Closest Subway: Jourdain
Address: 101, Rue des Couronnes, 75020 Paris

4. La Bellevilloise

La Bellevilloise got its name from a Parisian cooperative of the same name founded in 1877, which offered political education, culture, and a place of resistance to modest people from 1910 to 1949. Now it competently multitasks as a bar, restaurant, club, and exhibition space, hosting regular film and music festivals on the top level where there is a fake lawn with deck chairs and a massage area.

Creatives in Paris absolutely insist on checking out La Bellevilloise, a place many consider the best spot to experience the local music scene in Paris. Enjoy brunch in the Halle aux Oliviers or decent views of the quartier from the charming terrace. Downstairs, the club/concert venue has launched some of Paris's most exciting new bands. A very cool place to visit, especially for Sunday brunch!

Hours: Wednesday - Friday (7:00 pm - 2:00 am), Saturday (11:00 am - 6:00 am), and Sunday (11:00 am - 1:00 am). Closed Monday and Tuesday.
Price Range: €8 - €20
Closest Subway: Gambetta
Address: 19-21 Rue Boyer, 75020 Par

5. Lou Pascalou

Known as a cafe and an art space, Lou Pascalou has also been appropriated as a neighborhood canteen thanks to its endlessly inventive nature. It is a sweetly boho chic hangout with youthful local clientele. The drinks are super cheap, and so is the food. There is also a wide range of entertainment every night of the week. On weekends, the bar is packed so do not arrive too late if you want to be able to find a place to sit.

Hours: Monday - Sunday (2:00 pm - 2:00 am).
Price Range: €8 - €20
Closest Subway: Ménilmontant
Address: 14 Rue des Panoyaux, 75020 Paris

6. Bistrot Blanc Bec

Bistrot Blanc Bec is somewhat a hidden bistro not often frequented by tourists, but locals sure love it. It is a cozy place with a warm, Southern French ambiance and a fresh, creative menu.

Hours: Tuesday - Saturday for brunch (9:00 am - 2:30 pm) and dinner (7:30 pm - 11:00 pm).
Price Range: €21 - €40
Closest Subway: Ménilmontant
Address: 15 rue des Panoyaux, 75020

7. Le Lion Indomptable

Le Lion Indomptable is a Cameroonian restaurant owned by Marcel 'Le Lion' Boum. Here, you will most certainly try authentic dishes of Cameroonian cuisine, listen to Cameroonian music, and drink some killer Ginger rum drinks Boum mixes himself. The cheery facade and vibrant interior with green Moroccan banquettes, animal-print upholstery, and Cameroonian artwork make this place incredibly exciting! Guests can try dishes like maffes and yassas from Senegal, ndole, mbongo tjobi, or a choice of meat or fish in gombo sauce, plantains, and rice. Yum!

Hours: Sunday - Tuesday (7:30 pm - 2:00 am), and Wednesday - Saturday (12:00 pm - 3:30 pm).
Price Range: €7 - €20
Closest Subway: Alexandre Dumas
Address: 86 Rue de la Réunion, 75020 Paris

8. Le Rouleau de Printemps

Le Rouleau de Printemps never disappoints, with its reliable quality and disarming simplicity. You cannot reserve a place in one of the two postcard-sized rooms, so arrive early to get a space at the shared tables. A coriander-scented bo bun, some plump, crunchy egg rolls, a vegetarian spring roll, and some steamed prawn ravioli washed down with jasmine tea or Tsingtao beer will not cost you much more than €20, but go easy on the ordering -- sometimes the service can be chaotic. The staff are always charming but the dishes arrive haphazardly, sometimes poorly presented, as and when they are finished by the matron in the kitchen; but at these prices, it would hardly do to complain.

Hours: Monday - Sunday for lunch (12:00 pm - 3:00 pm) and dinner (7:00 pm - 12:00 am).
Price Range: €5 - €10
Closest Subway: Belleville
Address: 42 Rue de Tourtille, 75020 Paris

9. L'Abribus

A Moroccan-themed restaurant serving some of the best couscous in town according to many travel guides, L'Abribus is a great place to escape the crowds and share plates with family or friends. The portions are incredibly big, so sharing is definitely recommended. With a great atmosphere, a good balance between delicious French and Moroccan cuisine, and reasonable prices, this place is certainly a must-visit.

Hours: Monday - Sunday (7:00 am - 2:00 am).
Price Range: €7 - €12
Closest Subway: Alexandre Dumas
Address: 56 Rue de Bagnolet, 75020 Paris

10. Roseval

The earnest young duo behind Roseval produces a suite of tasty portions focused on produce which are aesthetically studied and cautiously sensual. Even before the first dish arrives at the table, thought, you will love the brilliantly funky venue — a small and slightly ramshackle old tavern named after a small red-skinned variety of potato. The winsomely charming service by Erica Biswell, the lovely Colombian sommelier, and Clément Boutreux, previously a waiter at Le Bistrot Paul Bert, are sure to impress.

Hours: Monday - Friday (8:00 pm - 12:00 am). Closed Saturday and Sunday.
Price Range: €20 - €60
Closest Subway: Ménilmontant (2)
Address: 1 Rue d'Eupatoria, 75020 Paris

5 Paris Street Foods You Can Try:

In the past, eating while walking along the street or sitting on a park bench used to be looked down upon in France. Eating was supposed to be enjoyed in restaurants or sidewalk cafes. Today, however, times have changed, and eating street food has become an acceptable concept. Today, you will see people happily grubbing on anything from sandwiches to kebabs, empanadas to pizza, falafels to crepes, without ever breaking the bank while strolling along the Parisian streets.

Here are some winning street foods that you can grab on your trip, as well as the best places to get them.

1. Crepes

You cannot come to France without trying the famous crepes. Stop for crepes at a booth on a sidewalk -- you can find them all over the city. Many cafes and restaurants also have crepe booths that sell freshly-made crepes. You can choose from plain and simple with some butter and sugar, to fancier crepes filled with chocolate and nuts, ham and cheese, apricot jam, as well as many other options that may tickle your fancy. Places like Josselin (14th Arrondissement), Creperie Bretonne (11th Arrondissement), Breizh Cafe (3rd Arrondissement), and West Country Girl (11th Arrondissement), have some amazing on-the-go crepes you can try!

Josselin: 67 Rue du Montparnasse, 75014 Paris (Closest Subway Station: Vavin)

Crêperie Bretonne: 67 Rue de Charonne, 75011 Paris (Closest Subway Station: Charonne)

Breizh Café: 111 Rue Vieille du Temple, 75003 Paris (Closest Subway Station: Charonne)

West Country Girl: 6 Passage Saint-Ambroise, 75011 Paris (Closest Subway Station: Rue Saint Maur)

2. Kebabs

A great Mediterranean fast-food option in Paris is Lebanese food. A juicy piece of meat and veggies on a stick - what's not to love? A kebab is a perfect food choice in the wee hours of the night between clubbing and bedtime. It is on a stick, it is not messy, and it will help you restore some sobriety. Istanbul in the 17th Arrondissement and Daily Syrien in the 10th Arrondissement are your best options.

Istanbul: Rue des Batignolles, 75017 Paris (Closest Subway Station: Batignolles)

Daily Syrien: 55 Rue du Faubourg Saint-Denis, 75010 Paris (Closest Subway Station: Château d'eau)

3. Burgers

Parisians have officially gone burger-crazy. After the Camion qui Fume (a mobile gourmet burger van) made its debut in December 2012, burger joints and burger trucks have been popping up all over the city. The burgers include a wide variety of meats and options. Le Camion qui Fume (but often near the Movie Theater MK2 at BNF) and Cantine California are never in the same place, so you have to track them down online. Another awesome joint that does stay put is Big Fernand, an ultra-trendy take-away joint in the 10th.

Big Fernand: 32 Rue Saint-Sauveur, 75002 Paris (Closest Subway Station: Sentier)

4. Pizzas

Ah, pizza! It is a classic favorite, perfect for any occasion, at any time of day. Thick, gooey, cheesy goodness that melts in your mouth and is perfect if you are on the go. There is a plethora of pizza spots where you can get on-the-go pizza, but Le Camion à Pizzas, a mobile pizza van in central Paris, is the best place to get some quick, delicious pizza. Its shiny black, retro-futurist bodywork looks like something from 'pimp my ride," and it blends in perfectly with the wacky art installation on display all around.

Le Camion à Pizzas: 104 rue d'Aubervilliers, 75019 Paris (Closest Subway Station: Stalingrad)

5. Falafel

Falafel may not be French, but it is probably the most desired fast food item in Paris. A string of always packed restaurants along the Rue des Rosiers in the traditional Jewish quarter of the Marais district have become extremely popular among tourists, and for good reason: soft, thick pita bread is filled with perfectly crisp chickpea balls and complemented with a variety of freshly cut vegetables, tahini, hummus and hot sauce. L'A's du Falafel (4th), Chez Hanna (4th), Comptoir Mediterranee (5th), and Maoz Falafel (6th) are all great options!

L'A's du Falafel: 32-34 Rue des Rosiers, 75004 Paris (Closest Subway Station: Saint Paul)

Chez Hanna: 54 Rue des Rosiers, 75004 Paris (Closest Subway Station: Saint Paul)

Comptoir Méditerranée: 42 Rue du Cardinal Lemoine, 75005 Paris (Closest Subway Station: Cardinal Lemoine)

Maoz Falafel: 8 Rue Xavier Privas, 75005 Paris (Closest Subway Station: Saint Michel)

Must-try Meals/Dishes In Paris:

France is home to a lot of wonderful dishes, and while there, you should definitely not miss out on these. Here is a list of the must-try foods and the best places to go.

Meals/Dishes	Restaurants/Bistros

1. Croque Monsieur   –   Le Terroir Parisien

This is an enjoyable grilled ham and cheese usually served with Gruyere or Emmental cheese. When served with a fried or poached egg on top, it becomes Croque Madame. It is often served for lunch and is absolutely a treat.

Le Terroir Parisien: 20 Rue Saint-Victor, 75005 Paris (Closest Subway Station: Maubert - Mutualité)

2. Salade Nicoise   –   Reparate

This soul-nourishing salad contains tuna, anchovies, green beans, tomato wedges, hard-boiled eggs, sliced potatoes, and black olives, and is dressed in a tasty vinaigrette. It has become a staple salad in most brasseries.

Reparate: 128 Rue de Charenton, 75012 Paris (Closest Subway Station: Reuilly Diderot)

3. Escargot   –   Le Réveil du 10ème

These slimy little critters are made entirely appetizing with some butter and usually some garlic and parsley. They are much easier to eat than you would imagine. Snails are something to try when in Paris as an appetizer, just to see what all the fuss is about.

Le Réveil du 10e : 35 Rue du Château d'Eau, 75010 Paris (Closest Subway Station: Château d'eau)

4. Brandade de Morue   –   Chez Janou

A Provencal dish found on many menus in Paris. Brandade de Morue is mashed salt cod blended with olive oil and garlic until it becomes a smooth cream, often mixed in with whipped potatoes. This is a perfect dish on a cold day.
Chez Janou: 2 Rue Roger Verlomme, 75003 Paris (Closest Subway Station: Chemin Vert)

5. Chèvre chaud   –   L'Arsenal

This is a winning combination of shallot vinaigrette, tomatoes, and hot little rounds of melted goat cheese on bread.

L'Arsenal: 2 Rue de Birague, 75004 Paris (Closest Subway Station: Saint Paul)

6.   Falafel   –   L'As Du Falafel

Although not by any means a quintessentially Parisian food, falafels are a must-try food item in Paris. A falafel is a deep-fried ball or patty made from ground chickpeas, fava beans, or both. It is usually served in a pita, or wrapped in a flatbread, then drizzled with delicious tahini-based sauce.

L'A's du Falafel: 32-34 Rue des Rosiers, 75004 Paris (Closest Subway Station: Saint Paul)

7.   Confit de Canard   –   Au Trou gascon

Duck leg cooked in its own fat, Confit de Canard is an incredibly popular dish among the French. Usually served with roasted potatoes, this dish is tender and flavorful. What's not to love about it?

Au Trou gascon: 40 Rue Taine, 75012 Paris (Closest Subway Station: Daumesnil)

8.   Cassoulet   –   l'Assiette

The cassoulet is a rich, slow-cooked casserole containing meat (typically pork sausages, goose, duck, and sometimes mutton), pork skin, and white beans. This is a winter favorite among Parisians.

l'Assiette: 181 Rue du Château, 75014 Paris (Closest Subway Station: Denfert Rochereau)

9.   Steak tartare   –   Severo

Instead of getting cooked beef, why not try the fresher version? Steak tartare is raw ground beef mixed with various seasonings and a raw egg. It sounds gross, but it is actually tastier than it sounds!

Severo: 8 Rue des Plantes, 75014 Paris (Closest Subway Station: Alesia)

10.   Boeuf Bourguignon   –   Chez Josephine Dumonet

A favorite dish in the winter months, boeuf bourguignon is a slow-cooked beef stew with an enormous quantity of Burgundy wine poured into the sauce. It pairs perfectly with a glass of French red wine.

Chez Josephine Dumonet: 117 Rue du Cherche-Midi, 75006 Paris (Closest Subway Station: Duroc)

11.   Quiche Lorraine   –   Angelina

Quiche Lorraine is a quiche made with egg, cream, cheese, and bits of ham. It can be served hot or cold.

Angelina: 19 Rue de Vaugirard, 75006 Paris (Closest Subway Station: Rennes)

12. Galettes   –   Breizh café

Galettes are similar to the popular crepe except they are made with buckwheat instead. It is usually served with your choice of fillings -- it can be eaten savory or sweet. It is also great for tourists who are looking for something gluten-free.

Breizh café: 111 Rue Vieille du Temple, 75003 Paris (Closest Subway Station: Saint Sebastien Froissart)

13. Steak frites   –   Café des Musées

This is one of those dishes people have heard of before visiting Paris but may think is something more complicated than it actually is. It is a steak and fries – and that is essentially it! Entrecote is usually the type of steak used in this meal.

Café des Musées: 49 Rue de Turenne, 75003 Paris (Closest Subway Station: Chemin Vert)

14. Coq au Vin   –   A la Biche au Bois

A perfect cold weather favorite among Parisians, this is a chicken dish braised with wine, bacon, mushrooms, and sometimes garlic. The wine typically used is Burgundy.

A la Biche au Bois: 45 Avenue Ledru-Rollin, 75012 Paris (Closest Subway Station: Ledru-Rollin)

15. Moules/Mussels   –   Le Baratin

When they are in season, you will see signs for moules (mussels) on sidewalk chalkboards in front of restaurants all over Paris. They are a Parisian must-have, and worth trying even if you have had mussels in other places. For a variation, try "mouclade," which is a dish of mussels baked in a cream and white wine sauce.

Le Baratin: 41 Boulevard Saint-Marcel, 75013 Paris (Closest Subway Station: Saint Marcel)

16. Huitres/Oysters   –   La Cabane à Huîtres

Like mussels, huitres (oysters) are also a popular shellfish among Parisians when in season.

La Cabane à Huîtres: 4 Rue Antoine Bourdelle, 75015 Paris (Closest Subway Station: Falguière)

17. Onion soup   –   Brasserie Mollard

This is a rich beef-based broth full of onions cooked until they are soft and sweet, then covered with cheese and baked in the oven. It is absolutely delicious, and very filling!

Brasserie Mollard: 115 Rue Saint-Lazare, 75008 Paris (Closest Subway Station: Havre-Caumartin)

18. Foie gras – Bistro Volnay

Foie gras is a luxury food product made of the liver of a duck or goose that has been specially fattened. It is usually served with toast, jam, and coarse salt, and is the perfect way to start a meal or to indulge with a glass of wine.

Bistro Volnay: 8 Rue Volney, 75002 Paris (Closest Subway Station: Madeleine)

19. Oeuf mayo – l'Evasion

This is essentially hard-boiled eggs with mayonnaise. The dish is usually served as a starter.

l'Evasion: 7 Place Saint-Augustin, 75008 Paris (Closest Subway Station: Saint-Augustin)

20. Sole meunière – Le Duc

Sole meuniere is a classic French dish that consists of sole (whole or fillet) that is dredged in milk and flour, then fried in butter and served with the resulting buttery brown sauce and lemon. This is great with a glass of Chardonnay!

Le Duc: 243 Boulevard Raspail, 75014 Paris (Closest Subway Station: Raspail)

Must-try Pastries In Paris:

In Paris, you have the perfect opportunity to taste the sweet, buttery perfection of some of the best pastries the world has to offer. Parisian pastry chefs are famed for their skills, which they train long and hard to hone in order to craft pastries that can take you to heaven with every bite.

Here is a list of 10 irresistible Parisian pastry superstars and recommendations for where to devour them in France's capital city.

Pastries		Bakeries

1.   Macarons   –   **Café Pouchkine | Laduree | Pierre Hermé**

These small, round treats are made with almonds and come in a plethora of delicious flavors. They are sandwiched together with ganache, buttercream and jam. The vivid colors that make macarons so appealing are a feast for the eyes as much as a treat for your taste buds.

Café Pouchkine: 155 Boulevard Saint-Germain, 75006 Paris (Closest Subway Station: Saint-Germain des Près)
Ladurée: 43 Rue de Varenne, 75007 Paris (Closest Subway Station: Rue du Bac)
Pierre Hermé: 18 Rue Sainte-Croix de la Bretonnerie 75004 (Closest Subway Station: Saint Paul)

2.   Tarte Caramel Salé   –   **Sadaharu AOKI**

This is a buttery, crumbly crust cupping a gooey pool of salty caramel, all crowned with a swirling milk chocolate creme that has been artfully dusted in cocoa.
Sadaharu AOKI: 35 Rue de Vaugirard, 75006 Paris (Closest Subway Station: Rennes)

3.   Éclairs   –   **L'Éclair de Génie | Fauchon | Jacques Genin**

Airy choux pastry filled with cream and topped with fondant, the éclair defines French pastries and fills bakeries all around Paris. Fillings and toppings such as chocolate, caramel, or coffee comprise the traditional éclair, but these classic tastes have also made way for more modern twists with artful decorations and intriguing flavors.

L'Éclair de Génie: 32 Rue Notre Dame des Victoires 75002 (Closest Subway Station: Bourse)
Fauchon: 26 Place de la Madeleine, 75008 Paris (Closest Subway Station: Madeleine)
Jacques Genin: 133 Rue de Turenne, 75003 Paris (Closest Subway Station: Filles du Calvaire)

4.   Tarte au Chocolat   –   **Gosselin | Pierre Hermé**

Want to feed your chocolate fix without having to order a "dainty" and "delicate" truffle? Go for the tarte au chocolat. Velvety chocolate ganache goodness is poured into a flaky shell and solidifies to the texture of fudge.

Gosselin: 125 Rue Saint Honoré, 75001 Paris (Closest Subway Station: Saint Michel)

Pierre Hermé: 18 Rue Sainte-Croix de la Bretonnerie 75004 (Closest Subway Station: Louvre Rivoli)

5.   Tarte Tatin   –   Crèmerie Restaurant Polidor | Au Pied de Fouet

Caramelized apple cooked to a golden brown sugary sweetness is the most important ingredient in the tarte tatin. Cooked in a pan with the pastry on top, this dish results in an upside down feature of glory when served on a plate. You can eat this deliciousness cold, but it is even better when eaten warm with a spoonful of tart creme fraiche.

Crèmerie Restaurant Polidor: 41 Rue Monsieur le Prince, 75006 Paris (Closest Subway Station: Cluny Sorbonne)
Au Pied de Fouet: 5 Rue Saint-Benoît, 75006 Paris (Closest Subway Station: Saint Germain des Près)

6.   Mille-feuille   –   Pierre Hermé | La Patisserie des Reves

Meaning "thousand sheets," mille-feuille is a flaky puff pastry with layers alternating with sweet cream filling. Icing sugar or fondant is spread on top and topped with chocolate.

Pierre Hermé: 18 Rue Sainte-Croix de la Bretonnerie (Closest Subway Station: Louvre Rivoli)
La Patisserie des Rêves: 93 Rue du Bac, 75007 Paris (Closest Subway Station: Rue du Bac)

7.   Choux à la crème   –   Odette | Pain de Sucre

These delightful rounds of hollow pastries are commonly filled with cream and covered with gooey chocolate to create a profiterole. But flavors can vary as can toppings, from ice cream to spun caramel, fruit, and frostings. Piled high, they create the famous Parisian wedding cake, "the croquembouche."

Odette: 77 Rue Galande, 75005 Paris (Closest Subway Station: Saint Michel)

Pain de Sucre: 24 Rue de Turenne, 75003 Paris (Closest Subway Station: Chemin Vert)

8.   Caramels   –   Jacques Genin | Patrick Roger

These treats are so soft and buttery, you wonder how they manage to keep their shape. Classic caramels like the salty butter caramels are a favorite among Parisians, but other decadent options include flavors like pistachio, almond, hazelnut, coffee, vanilla, ginger, and cinnamon. Most people tell themselves they will only eat one, but once you have one, you will not be able to stop!

Jacques Genin: 133 Rue de Turenne, 75003 Paris (Closest Subway Station: Filles du Calvaire)
Patrick Roger: 108 Boulevard Saint-Germain, 75006 Paris (Closest Subway Station: Odeon)

9.   Pain au Chocolat   –   Angelina Patisserie | Pierre Hermé | Eric Kayser

Pain au chocolat is made of the same layered dough as a croissant. It is golden and slightly crispy on the outside, with one or two pieces of melted chocolate swirled throughout the buttery pastry inside. This is often sold still hot, or at least warm, from the oven!

Angelina Patisserie: 226 Rue de Rivoli, 75001 Paris (Closest Subway Station: Tuileries)

Pierre Hermé: 18 Rue Sainte-Croix de la Bretonnerie (Closest Subway Station: Louvre Rivoli)

Eric Kayser: 4 Rue de l'Échelle, 75001 Paris (Closest Subway Station: Palais Royal- Musée du Louvre)

10.   L'opera cake   –   Dalloyau

This elegant cake is comprised of thin layers of biscuit Viennois soaked in coffee syrup and then layered with coffee-flavored buttercream and chocolate ganache. It is assembled as a large square or rectangle and then cut into large bar-shaped slices to serve and enjoy on-the-go.

Dalloyau: 63 Rue de Grenelle, 75007 Paris (Closest Subway Station: Rue du Bac)

10 Best Gluten-Free Restaurants In Paris:

Nowhere in France is there more restaurants than in Paris, and whether you suffer from Celiac Disease, gluten-intolerance, or simply prefer to follow a gluten-free diet, it can be difficult when you do not know where to go.

Here is a list of some of the best places to eat that Paris can offer a gluten-free traveler.

1. NoGlu

As the name suggests, this restaurant is entirely gluten free. Noglu is a restaurant that serves classic French cuisine and desserts, all gluten-free! Noglu is open for lunch and brunch during the day and has a fixed menu Wednesday through Friday nights. Reservations are recommended. Do not forget to try the amazing caramelized apple crumble for dessert!

Hours: Monday - Friday (12:00 pm - 3:00 pm), Wednesday - Friday (3:00 pm - 6:30 pm), Thursday - Saturday (7:30 pm - 11:00 pm) and Saturday (11:00 am - 3:00 pm). Closed Sunday.
Price Range: €21 - €40
Closest Subway Station: Richelieu - Drouot
Address: 53 Passage des Panoramas, 75002 Paris

2. Helmut Newcake

This is the first 100% certified gluten-free bakery in Paris. Those looking to enjoy authentic French pastries like classic éclairs and lemon meringue tarts can stop in and take a seat in the modern yet cozy loft-style shop for a cup of coffee and a snack. From Wednesday to Saturday, owners François and Marie Tagliaferro offer inexpensive gluten-free lunch options like simple soups, salads, and quiches. The bakery also stocks gluten-free goods from England not typically found in France, so do a bit of shopping while you are at it.

Hours: Wednesday - Saturday (12:00 pm - 8:00 pm), Sunday (10:00 am - 6:00 pm). Closed Monday and Tuesday.
Price Range: Under €10
Closest Subway Station: Goncourt
Address: 53 Passage des Panoramas, 75002 Paris

3. Breizh Cafe

If you're in the mood for a crepe, try Breizh cafe. Famous for their gluten-free gallettes (crepes made with buckwheat), the choice of fillings are fairly limited, but the ingredients are of high quality, including the use of Valrhona chocolate with 70% cocoa solids in the dessert crepes.

Hours: Wednesday - Sunday (11:30 am - 11:00 pm). Closed Monday and Tuesday.
Price Range: €7 - €20
Closest Subway Station: Saint-Sébastien – Froissart
Address: 53 Passage des Panoramas, 75002 Paris

4. Biosphere Café

Biosphère Café is a dedicated gluten-free, homemade, and organic creperie (except the meat). They offer items like fresh baked baguettes, pizza, soups, quiches, macaroons and some pastries also come gluten and dairy-free.

Hours: Monday - Friday (12:00 pm - 6:00 pm), Saturday (12:00 pm - 10:00 pm). Closed Sunday.
Price Range: €1.50 - €15
Closest Subway Station: Saint Augustin
Address: 53 Passage des Panoramas, 75002 Paris

5. Maceo

With its great location opposite the gardens of the Palais Royal, Maceo sets out to lure you in from the get-go. Maceo offers a wide range of gluten-free options and has an excellent "green menu" as well, with some of the best vegetarian food in Paris. Also, if you contact them before visiting, they may even create a special gluten-free menu for you!

Hours: Monday - Friday (12:00 pm - 2:30 pm), Monday - Saturday (7:30 pm - 10:45 pm). Closed Sunday.
Price Range: €30 - €50
Closest Subway Station: Pyramides (7, 14)
Address: 53 Passage des Panoramas, 75002 Paris

6. Spring

Spring is owned by American chef Daniel Rose, and is not exactly a 100% gluten-free restaurant. However, Spring is very used to accommodating coeliacs. They also offer very delicious gluten-free bread.
Hours: Tuesday - Saturday (6:30 pm - 10:30 pm). Closed Sunday and Monday.

Price Range: €50 - €100

Closest Subway Station: Louvre-Rivoli (1)

Address: 53 Passage des Panoramas, 75002 Paris

7. Brasserie Balzar

Brasserie Balzar has wonderful food and a great atmosphere. It requires more formal attire but is truly a great place to dine in the Latin Quarter or for brunch after services at Notre Dame. If you are with a group and one of your group members has celiac, this is a great place, as it offers naturally gluten-free options on the menu.
Hours: Sunday (8:30 am - 10:30 pm), Monday - Saturday (8:30 am - 11:00 pm).

Price Range: €8 - €50
Closest Subway Station: Cluny- La Sorbonne
Address: 53 Passage des Panoramas, 75002 Paris

8. Aux Ducs De Bourgogne

Like Breizh Café, Aux Ducs De Bourgogne serves some great galettes. The Lebanese owner named Charles is very animated and willing to help you choose the best crepe for your taste buds. This is also a great place if you are looking to dine on a budget!

Hours: Monday - Friday (11:30 pm - 3:00 pm and 7:00 pm - 10:00 pm). Closed Sunday.
Price Range: €11 - €20
Closest Subway Station: Varenne
Address: 53 Passage des Panoramas, 75002 Paris

9. Café Pinson

Café Pinson is another addition to the trend of high quality healthy restaurants in Paris that do vegetarian and organic food with a bit of glamor. A comfortable, welcoming venue in the Marais, it offers carefully thought-out vegetarian, organic, and gluten-free dishes that are above ordinary. The menu changes daily, as does the energetic detox juice drink that is recommended to go with your meal.

Hours: Sunday (10:00 am - 6:00 pm), Monday - Friday (9:00 am - 12:00 am), and Saturday (10:00 am - 12:00 am).
Price Range: €11 - €20
Closest Subway Station: Filles du Calvaire (8)
Address: 53 Passage des Panoramas, 75002 Paris

10. Tugalik

The motto here translates roughly as: fill yourself with good food and flourish. The place is a cool, modern space in shades of white, beige, and brown with wooden tables. The menu features vegetarian and gluten-free dishes like pumpkin soup with coconut milk and quinoa risotto with legumes. Absolutely delicious!

Hours: Monday - Saturday (11:30 am - 10:30 pm). Closed Sunday.
Price Range: €11 - €20
Closest Subway Station: Cluny - La Sorbonne
Address: 53 Passage des Panoramas, 75002 Paris

10 Best Vegetarian Restaurants In Paris:

Do not let anyone tell you Paris does not cater to vegetarian and vegan diets! If you know where to look, delicious, wholesome goodness is easily available. Dig a little deeper and you will discover a limited yet flourishing vegetarian restaurant scene.

1. Macéo

With its great location opposite the gardens of the Palais Royal, Maceo sets out to lure you from the get-go. Maceo offers a wide range of vegetarian options with its excellent "green menu." Here is where you can try some of the best vegetarian food you have ever tasted. You will not be presented with a bland vegetable platter, either: here, the Japanese-born chef treats his vegetarian creations as just as important as his meat creations.

Hours: Monday - Friday (12:00 pm - 2:30 pm), Monday - Saturday (7:30 pm - 10:45 pm). Closed Sunday for the whole day and Saturday for lunch.
Price Range: €21 - €49
Closest Subway Station: Pyramides (7, 14)
Address: 53 Passage des Panoramas, 75002 Paris

2. L'Arpège

With three Michelin stars, this place is legendary in the restaurant world. Chef Alain Passard creates phenomenal dishes using produce grown in one of his three gardens. But, be prepared to spend some cash here.
Hours: Monday - Friday (12:00 pm - 2:30 pm) and (7:00 pm - 10:30 pm). Closed Saturday and Sunday.
Price Range: Above €41
Closest Subway Station: Varenne (13)
Address: 53 Passage des Panoramas, 75002 Paris

3. Soya Cantine

Soya has a French sense of style despite serving very un-French food. Simple yet elegant wooden tables are shared with other diners, giving the place a convivial atmosphere that is helped by the relaxed and amiable staff. Try the wonderfully light vegetarian lasagne and the apple crumble with roasted hazelnuts and orange zest. If you want to try vegan dessert, phone ahead.

Hours: Monday - Saturday (12:00 am - 3:30 pm) and (6:45 pm - 11:00 pm); Sunday (12:00 - 3:30 pm).
Price Range: €11 - €20
Closest Subway Station: Goncourt (11)
Address: 53 Passage des Panoramas, 75002 Paris

4. Gentle Gourmet Cafe

This is a vegan restaurant, cafe, deli, and boutique. Gentle Gourmet Cafe serves a variety of French and Mediterranean dishes both classic and contemporary. They also offer raw and gluten-free options as well. This classy bistro atmosphere lends itself to casual as well as special dining, and also has a Book crossing Zone where you can pick up free books to read!

Hours: Tuesday - Sunday (11:00 am - 2:00 pm) and (6:00 pm - 10:00 pm). Closed Monday.
Price Range: €21 - €40
Closest Subway Station: Quai de la Rapée (10,5)
Address: 53 Passage des Panoramas, 75002 Paris

5. Grand Appétit

Grand Appetit is a pioneer in the vegetarian eating scene, dating back to the mid-80s. This restaurant is attached to an organic supermarket in the Marais district. Those looking for an elegant veggie experience can forget about it here. Grand Appétit is a solution for those looking to avoid meat but also milk, eggs, and sugar. It is healthy, fresh, affordable, and it definitely attracts a certain type of health-conscious diner. Do not forget to clear your table afterwards, though!

Hours: Monday - Thursday (12:00 pm - 9:00 pm) and Friday (12:00 pm - 2:00 pm). Closed Saturday and Sunday.
Price Range: €11 - €20
Closest Subway Station: Bastille (1,5,8)
Address: 53 Passage des Panoramas, 75002 Paris

6. Le Grenier de Notre Dame

A 5-minute walk from the Notre Dame Cathedral, Le Grenier de Notre Dame is a quaint two-floor restaurant. Serving lunch and dinner, the set menu provides good choices for vegetarians and vegans alike, like skewered seitan, lentil moussaka, tofu ravioli, and vegetarian paella. The juices are highly recommended, too!

Hours: Sunday - Saturday (12:00 pm - 11:00 pm).
Price Range: €11 - €20
Closest Subway Station: Maubert - Mutualité (10)
Address: 53 Passage des Panoramas, 75002 Paris

7. Café Pinson

Café Pinson has a nice, cozy atmosphere paired with tasty vegan selections. This place is a must-go for those with dietary restrictions and those aiming to eat healthy.

Hours: Sunday (10:00 am - 6:00 pm), Monday - Friday (9:00 am - 12:00 am) and Saturday (10:00 am - 12:00 am).
Price Range: €11 - €20
Closest Subway Station: Filles du Calvaire
Address: 6 rue du Forez, 75003 Paris

8. Au Grain de Folie

Possibly the smallest and most intimate of Parisian veggie restaurants, Au Grain de Folie is a homey vegetarian restaurant in the Montmartre district. This is an interesting experience, to say the least, but will please those with a more traditional veggie palette who are looking for a healthy, balanced meal. Au Grain de Folie serves wholesome organic fare at reasonable prices, but make sure to call ahead to secure a table.

Hours: Monday - Friday (1:30 pm - 3:00 pm) and (7:30 pm - 10:30 pm), and Saturday - Sunday (12:30 pm - 10:30 pm).
Price Range: €11 - €20
Closest Subway Station: Abbesses (12)
Address: 53 Passage des Panoramas, 75002 Paris

9.   Le Potager du Marais

This is a very small, rustic Paris vegan restaurant decorated with lush flora that has been in business since 2012. Le Potager du Marais serves French cuisine but in vegan versions like hot soups, homemade tofu, and seitan bourguignon. There is also a pastry chef that prepares vegan-style pastries like blueberry bundt. The atmosphere at Le Potager du Marais is fun and homey; reservations are recommended to guarantee seating.
Hours: Wednesday - Sunday (12:00 pm - 4:00 pm) and (7:00 pm - 12:00 am).
Price Range: €21 - €40
Closest Subway Station: Rambuteau (11)
Address: 53 Passage des Panoramas, 75002 Paris

10. Le Marais

Formerly called Aquarius, Le Marais restaurant is one of the best-known among the Paris vegetarian community. The menu is a combination of salads, wheat pancakes, and savory tarts, with fish dishes also being featured. Vegans should check with wait staff before ordering, as some dishes contain egg and other non-vegan ingredients.

Hours: Monday - Saturday (12:00 pm - 2:15 pm) and (7:00 pm - 10:30 pm). Closed Sunday.
Price Range: €11 - €20
Closest Subway Station: Plaisance (13)
Address: 53 Passage des Panoramas, 75002 Paris

10 Restaurants for Kids/Family In Paris:

Eating out with children can be hectic, chaotic, and stressful. Some restaurants do not even cater to pint-sized guests. But, fear not! Hospitable Parisian hot spots, where kids are welcome and well catered for, do exist. Here is a list of 10 family-friendly restaurants to enjoy a stress-free family feast.

1. Relais d'Entrecote

At Le Relais de L'Entrecote, guests cannot help but love the endless amount of steak frites where the only option is, well, steak and fries covered in the restaurant's secret green herb sauce. Waitresses even come around with a second helping once the first is finished! Quick service and no-fuss food means a hassle-free meal for the whole family.
Hours: Sunday - Saturday (12:00 pm - 2:30 pm) and (7:00 pm - 11:30 pm).
Price Range: €20 - €34
Closest Subway Station: St. Germain des Pres (4)
Address: 53 Passage des Panoramas, 75002 Paris

2. Breizh Café

What kid does not love a delicious crepe? Breizh Café's well-sourced products are of high quality, which puts it way above most creperies. Breizh Cafe is a perfect place to enjoy savory or sweet crepes with the whole family.

Hours: Sunday (11:30 am - 10:00 pm) and Wednesday - Saturday (11:30 am - 11:00 pm).
Price Range: €11 - €20
Closest Subway Station: Saint-Sébastien - Froissart
Address: 53 Passage des Panoramas, 75002 Paris

3. Chez Hanna

Chez Hanna is a great spot to try some awesome falafels and shawarmas without having to wait in line like you would at L'As du Falafel. Chez Hanna remains something of the locals' secret, which is great for families who need space to eat. Prices are also incredibly affordable.

Hours: Tuesday - Sunday (11:30 am - 12:00 am). Closed Monday.
Price Range: €11 - €20
Closest Subway Station: Saint-Paul
Address: 53 Passage des Panoramas, 75002 Paris

4. Le Café du Marché

Frequented by locals and tourists alike, Le Cafe du Marche really is a hub of neighborhood activity, which is why it is great for families. The menu items such as the huge house salad featuring foie gras and parma ham is absolutely plentiful, delicious, and perfect for a family meal.

Hours: Sunday - Saturday (7:00 am - 1:00 am).
Price Range: €11 - €20
Closest Subway Station: École Militaire (8)

Address: 53 Passage des Panoramas, 75002 Paris

5. Baroche

Baroche is a cute, chic little restaurant. With its brick walls and old décor, you will feel like you are in a time warp in another century, making it fun for children. Also, it is open at all hours of the day, which is great for families with little ones who get hungry and tired at hours where most restaurants are closed.

Hours: Thursday - Friday (7:00 am - 2:00 am) and Saturday - Wednesday (7:00 am - 1:00 am). Closed Sunday.
Price Range: €11 - €20
Closest Subway Station: Saint-Philippe du Roule (9)
Address: 53 Passage des Panoramas, 75002 Paris

6. La Boule Rouge

La Boule Rouge has some of the most authentic couscous in Paris. The owner is from Tunisia, so you and your family will try some of the best North African family-style dishes here.

Hours: Monday - Saturday (12:00 pm - 3:00 pm) and (7:00 pm - 11:00 pm). Closed Sunday.
Price Range: €6 - €20
Closest Subway Station: Grands Boulevards
Address: 53 Passage des Panoramas, 75002 Paris

7. La Coupole

La Coupole in Montparnasse is the grandest of grand Parisian brasseries. An Art Deco triumph on an extraordinary scale, its famously vast dining room was once regularly graced by the top tiers of the artistic Rive Gauche set like Picasso, Jean-Paul Sartre, and Simone de Beauvoir. People still come here from all over the world to marvel at its splendour - all 1000 square meters and 33 pillars of it -- and to people watch, a timeless La Coupole pastime. The terrace tables in particular are perfect for watching life go by over a coffee and a crêpe Suzette. Because of its grand size, it is great for big families!

Hours: Sunday - Monday (8:30 am - 11:00 pm) and Tuesday - Saturday (8:30 am - 12:00 am).
Price Range: €20 - €40
Closest Subway Station: Vavin
Address: 53 Passage des Panoramas, 75002 Paris

8. Bistrot du Peintre

This art nouveau cafe-bistro is much loved by a laidback Bastille crowd for its satisfying, good-valued traditional cuisine and seasonal, market-inspired additions. Bistrot du Peintre is open all day, which is great when you are on vacation with young children.

Hours: Sunday (8:00 am - 2:00 am) and Monday - Saturday (7:00 am - 2:00 am).
Price Range: €11 - €20
Closest Subway Station: Ledru-Rollin (8)
Address: 53 Passage des Panoramas, 75002 Paris

9. Chez Clément

Chez Clement is a chain restaurant found all over the city, which brings affordable gourmet-like dining to its guests. The French menu varies with season, and includes dishes you would normally find at a super expensive restaurant, but at a fraction of the cost, making it very family-friendly.

Hours: Sunday - Saturday (11:00 am - 12:00 am).
Price Range: €8 - €20
Closest Subway Station: George V
Address: 53 Passage des Panoramas, 75002 Paris

10. Mama Shelter

This hip and trendy spot will surely be loved by the whole family. On the first floor, you will find a restaurant that serves simple, delicious dishes. There is also pizza available.
Hours: Monday - Sunday (11:00 am - 12:00 am).
Price Range: €21 - €40
Closest Subway Station: Porte de Bagnolet (3)
Address: 53 Passage des Panoramas, 75002 Paris

10 Best Restaurants For Less Than 15 Euros In Paris:

Traveling in France gets expensive, especially in Paris, but good food does not have to break the bank. Paris is filled with a plethora of amazing restaurants, and many of them you can find at affordable prices. Here is a list of 10 restaurants around Paris you can dine at on a budget.

1. L's du Falafel

Falafels! In a hurry and want something cheap and delicious? L'as du Falafel has just what you need. This is 'the' restaurant for falafels. L'as du Falafel is found in the Marais district and you can tell you are close by the number of people walking down the street holding falafels in their hands.

Hours: Monday - Thursday and Sunday (12:00 pm - 12:00 am), Friday (12:00 am - 4:00 pm), and Saturday (6:00 pm - 12:00 am).
Price Range: €7 - €10
Closest Subway Station: Saint-Paul
Address: 53 Passage des Panoramas, 75002 Paris

2. Le Petit Cler

Le Petit Cler is an excellent value for your money and great for a meal before heading off to see the Eiffel Tower. The menu is also vegetarian friendly. But the best part? The price. A different dish is served daily for only €12.50, and this includes amazing fare such as roast veal and even lovely steaks with potato and salad. This place is popular with locals, so remember to book early.

Hours: Monday - Sunday (8:00 am - 11:30 pm).
Price Range: €11 - €20
Closest Subway Station: École Militaire
Address: 29 rue Cler, 75007 Paris

3. Breizh Café

Breizh Café is a cozy little restaurant in the Marais district. It is a creperie unlike any other in Paris, and it is most definitely the spot to try amazingly priced crepes. Also, if you are looking for a gluten-free crepe (gallettes), this is definitely the spot to try them. Try both savory and sweet crepes and split the food (and cost) with another person.

Hours: Wednesday - Saturday (11:30 am - 11:00 pm) and Sunday (11:30 am - 10:00 pm). Closed Monday and Tuesday.
Price Range: €7 - €20
Closest Subway Station: Saint-Sébastien – Froissart
Address: 53 Passage des Panoramas, 75002 Paris

4. Le Nemrod

This cute little cafe is known for serving a delicious croque monsieur. A croque monsieur is essentially a ham and cheese sandwich. The croque madame takes it one step further by adding an egg on top, and Le Nemrod takes it lots of steps further with their amazing croque poilane. This deliciousness is under 15 Euros and will keep you full for hours!

Hours: Sunday - Saturday (7:00 am - 12:00 am).
Price Range: €11 - €20
Closest Subway Station: Rennes
Address: 53 Passage des Panoramas, 75002 Paris

5. Sol y Luna

What is not to love about Mexican food? Here, the food is cheap and cheerful, the vibe is sociable, and the decor is quirky. The weekday lunch menu offers you the best deal with a main course, dessert, and a coffee, all for 10 Euros! Awesome! Come early or you will not get a seat!

Hours: Sunday - Saturday (12:00 pm - 10:30 pm).
Price Range: €11 - €20
Closest Subway Station: Cluny - La Sorbonne
Address: 53 Passage des Panoramas, 75002 Paris

6. Frenchie to Go

Frenchie to Go lets you sample the highly-acclaimed cooking of Chef Gregory Marchard for a fraction of the price of its more upscale sibling, Bistro Frenchie. This cozy take-away or eat-in little shop offers sandwiches, cheesecake, doughnuts, and fish and chips for an average of €15 per person.

Hours: Monday - Friday (8:30 am - 4:30 pm), Saturday - Sunday (9:30 am - 5:30 pm).
Price Range: €11 - €20
Closest Subway Station: Sentier
Address: 9 rue du Nil, 75002 Paris

7. Cyclo

Named after a Vietnamese rickshaw, Cyclo's tiny room of just fifteen tables is a casual and inviting space. Prices for appetizers and main plates range from 5 to 11 Euros. Trying the bo bun is a must -- it is what makes guests always come back for more. For dessert, try the delicious steamed banana or creme brulee.

Hours: Monday - Saturday (12:00 pm - 2:30 pm) and (7:00 pm - 10:30 pm). Closed Sunday.
Price Range: €11 - €20
Closest Subway Station: Pyrénées
Address: 53 Passage des Panoramas, 75002 Paris

8. Café du Commerce

This spectacular restaurant has three floors! Serving mostly traditional French cuisine, regulars come here during the day to enjoy the incredibly affordable varied menu, as well as the very good set menu. You can also opt for a la carte salads or burgers for just 10 Euros. In the evenings during happy hour, locals flock here to enjoy some cheap drinks and snacks as well.

Hours: Sunday - Saturday (12:00 pm - 3:00 pm) and (7:00 pm - 12:00 am).
Price Range: €11 - €20
Closest Subway Station: Varenne
Address: 53 Passage des Panoramas, 75002 Paris

9. Chez Clément

Chez Clement is a chain restaurant found all over the city, which provides its guests with affordable, gourmet-like dining. The French menu varies with the season, and includes dishes you would normally find at a super expensive restaurant.

Hours: Sunday - Saturday (11:00 am - 12:00 am).
Price Range: €11 - €40
Closest Subway Station: George V
Address: 53 Passage des Panoramas, 75002 Paris

10. Rouleau de Printemps

For some cheap but filling and ever-so-trendy Chinese, Vietnamese, and other kinds of Asian food, this is the place to check out.

Hours: Monday - Tuesday (11:30 am - 3:00 pm) and (7:00 pm - 11:00 pm), Thursday - Sunday (11:30 am - 3:00 pm) and (7:00 pm to 11:00 pm). Closed Wednesday.
Price Range: €5 - €10
Closest Subway Station: Belleville
Address: 42 rue Tourtille, 75020 Paris

Conclusion

Paris is one of those very few cities in the world that can truly boast of having the most high-quality restaurants per square mile. Wherever you are in the city, there is bound to be a dining spot just waiting to blow your mind – and palate – away.

This staggering range of selections can be both a blessing and a curse to travelers. Given the usual tourist's limited period of time in Paris, it will be impossible to scour the endless array of food establishments in the city. With this book, however, you have a greater opportunity to explore the city's best places to dine at a budget of your choosing.

Paris for Foodies took you from the first Arrondissement to the twentieth, guiding you through Michelin-starred restaurants to a number of humble hole-in-the-wall joints. From the usual spots frequented by tourists to the hidden gems off the beaten path, take your pick in whichever district you find yourself in.

Any other tips?

As a matter of fact, there *is* more. I am tucking in here a few more tips to help you enjoy Parisian restaurants even more:

·   **Enjoy a leisurely meal.** When planning your vacation, make sure to factor in a couple hours or so for dining. A lovely meal should be unhurried! When you are in a rush to get to the next stop on your sightseeing list, it is more advisable for you to grab a quick bite in a café or a kiosk for a salad or sandwich. Otherwise, sit down for a three-course meal and linger over coffee or wine.

·   **Say hello to the pre fixe menu.** Parisians often order the fixed price meal which consists of the appetizer or entrée, main course or le plat principal, and le dessert. Not only are the fixed price menus carefully selected by the chef, they are also a good value for your money.

·   **Order wine to go with your meal.** Most Parisian restaurants have a wide selection of wines, and you can order a bottle with your meal. If you are unsure about which one to choose, you can always ask the waiter for recommendations on which wine complements the dishes you are ordering.

·   **Dial down the volume.** When dining in cafes or restaurants, make sure to speak softly. Space is at a premium in Paris, and tables are often placed very near to each other, so lower your voice while conversing!
Most important of all ---

·   **Loosen up and indulge!** For once, just forget about calories and enjoy a good meal. Try a cheese plate, a hefty three-course meal, and a trip to the patisserie, then gobble down a lovely pastry. You earned it after a day of walking around Paris!
French food is amazing.

You already know that, I know. But I cannot wait to take you further and help you appreciate French cuisine even more than you already do. The picturesque Parisienne cafes and restaurants are waiting for you.

And so... *Now what?*

Armed with this book, go ahead and enjoy a lovely time in Paris. If you need more help with your preparations, be sure to check out my website www.talkinfrench.com for more helpful guides, such as what to pack for your visit, the best sights to see, romantic places to take your sweetheart to, and loads of other free stuff.

You can also subscribe to my mailing list to be kept abreast of everything and anything French – from the language to culture, and everything in between.

Best of all, you can supplement this book with a wonderful phrase book that provides you with the right things to say in every possible scenario you will encounter during your visit in Paris. From your arrival at the airport to your sightseeing adventures, and, of course, dining, *Travel in France with Confidence* promises to give you exactly what the title suggests. It also has a MENU READER that will help you when you are ordering at the restaurants you choose. Kind of a match made in heaven, huh?

If you have any questions that have not been answered in this book, or if you want to reach me for any feedback or comments, do not hesitate to send me an email at frederic@talkinfrench.com. I try my best to respond to each email in as timely a manner as possible. All the best to you!

Merci!

Bonus book.

Paris for Selfies: The Best Spots for Photoshoots in Paris.

By Frederic Bibard
(talkinfrench.com)

INTRODUCTION

Paris is not just a city; it is a world on its own. Every little postcard-worthy nook and quaint corner is bursting with beauty and life, ready to be shot and immortalized in a photo.

The late, great Thomas Jefferson used to say, "A walk about Paris will provide lessons in history, beauty, and in the point of life." He was right. Paris will provide all of that, and a multitude of great spots for your family photos, your travel memories, or simply your Instagram feed.

This straightforward e-book will help you take the best photos on your Parisian holiday. By pointing you to the best places where you can pose for a selfie or snap a great architectural shot, this book is bound to be your bestie during your Parisian adventure. From the most iconic places like the Eiffel Tower to the lesser known locales, you will learn how to take the most amazing snapshots of stunning sceneries.

Aside from that, this e-book also offers a special treat for movie buffs and photography enthusiasts alike! See a list of 30 of the most famous movie locations all around Paris. Now you can recreate the scenes from your favorite films and visit the cafes featured in *Midnight in Paris*, the street where Amelie lived, and even the restaurant the Disney film *Ratatouille* was based on!

Here is a quick look at what you will find inside:

1. A list of the best photo shoot spots all over Paris, including tips about the area
2. Location details (nearest subway station and address)
3. A list of film locations and which movies were filmed there
4. More tips and other caption-worthy details

Are you ready to take the most jaw-dropping shots of Paris? Before you begin, here is a quick rundown of tips from photography pros to help take your travel photos from good to great, and from *so-so* to *WHOA!*

- When taking photos of familiar sites such as the Eiffel Tower, emphasize something aside from the subject. A good rule of thumb is to think of the simple definition of a noun (people, places, things) and incorporate all three into the photo. People – you or your family; places – the other areas you see; things – could be a good prop or something that will add depth to the photo.
- Be part of the action. Instead of just standing apart from the action, go ahead and join in – and get an awesome photo out of it! Being in the thick of things will make the photo more fun and action-filled, and will take it way above the mediocre travel photos littering your friends' social media feeds.
- Always consider the lighting. Check out where the sun is and make sure it is casting a favorable light on your subject. Ever tried taking a photo of a wonderful scene only to discover later on that the lighting was really bad? Do not let it cast a gloom over your Parisian memories!
- Sunrise and sunsets make for magical photos. The most striking images often happen when the world is bathed in golden sunlight. Take advantage of these moments!

- Look at the scene and divide it into three parts. The most interesting images can be taken when you consider the age-old rule of thirds. Mentally divide the sections of your frame into three (left, center, and right) and put the subject either in the left or right section or right in the middle of two sections. This is the easiest way to take compelling photos!
- Put your good sense of humor to use! Never underestimate the power of humor to turn an otherwise average photo into an outstanding one. So go ahead and have fun!
- Get crazy and creative! Do not let your photos fall into the pile of nondescript travel photos. Just pause to think for a while before snapping a shot and use your creative juices to take the most awesome shots!

And finally, the SELFIES!

Of course.you will need a perfectly good headshot from your lovely Parisian vacation. Before taking that selfie shot, remember these selfie ABC's!

A – Angle. You know your best angle, so work it! A also stands for Assess -- check out how you look, just quickly, to make sure you are looking fabulous (as I am sure you will!).

B – Background. You will find ample ideas for that in this book.

C – Check the lighting. The best way to take the most flattering shots is to put yourself in the best light. Natural light works best, too!

So are you ready to take on Paris? Yes, you are!

Have fun!

I.   The Best Photo Spots in Paris

1. The Eiffel Tower

This is a pretty obvious one and probably the first thing that everyone thinks of when Paris comes to mind. There are millions of great shots of the Eiffel Tower, both during the day and at night, and it is always worth getting your own! One thing to note is that the Eiffel Tower is pretty tall and dominates the Parisian skyline, meaning that great photos of the Eiffel Tower can be captured a good distance away. There are also plenty of parks and streets you can snap a picture from. You can also get up close to the tower and shoot from there - it is a great view!

Address: Champ de Mars, 5 Avenue Anatole France, 75007 Paris, France

Closest Subway Station: Champ de Mars, Tour Eiffel

photo source: https://en.wikipedia.org/wiki/Paris_syndrome

2. Notre Dame Cathedral

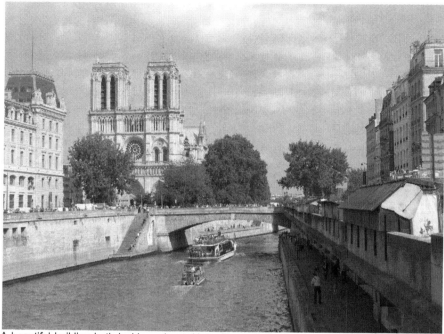

A beautiful building both inside and out, Notre Dame Cathedral is another spot that comes to mind when mentioning Paris. A great place to shoot from outside is down the riverbank of the Seine. The best time of day to take pictures is during the day when the light shines through the stained glass. You can also take a tour up to the top of one of the bell towers and take some amazing pictures of the view over the city. If you can stand the lines, go inside to take pictures too, but note that tripods are not allowed and the inside of the cathedral is pretty dark.

Address: 6 Parvis Notre-Dame - Pl. Jean-Paul II, 75004 Paris, France

Closest Subway Station: St Michel-Notre Dame

https://commons.wikimedia.org/wiki/File:Petit_Pont_and_Notre_Dame_Cathedral,_Paris_July_2014.jpg

3. The Louvre

The Louvre is another popular photo spot. The best time to take pictures outside of The Louvre is at night or early in the morning when it is not as crowded with tourists. There is the well-known main glass pyramid, a couple of smaller ones, and pretty reflecting pools, which make this place a great photo op. Tourists can also take pictures inside the museum, which is filled with all sorts of interesting and beautiful things to take pictures of.

Address: 75001 Paris, France
Closest Subway Station: Palais Royal - Musée du Louvre, Pont Neuf
https://en.wikipedia.org/wiki/File:Louvre_2007_02_24_c.jpg

4. Sainte Chapelle

Close to Notre Dame, Sainte Chapelle is incredibly beautiful inside and out. Inside, there are two parts to the chapel -- the lower section and the upper section. The lower section is where the entrance is where walls are pierced with smaller windows with distinctive spherical and triangular shapes. In the upper section, where all the famous stained glass resides, visitors will be wowed by its beauty. Sainte Chapelle is a great place to take some amazing pictures of stained glass.

Address: 8 Boulevard du Palais, 75001 Paris, France

Closest Subway Station: Saint-Michel
http://en.wikipedia.org/wiki/Sainte-Chapelle

5. The Arc de Triomphe du Carrousel

While not THE arc most readers are thinking of, it is still a pretty awesome arc to shoot. The Arc de Triomphe du Carrousel is richly decorated in rose marble on the columns and the front paneling. A plus is that it is a very short stroll from the entry of the Louvre, so it is an easy shot to get to before or after your museum visit. The best time to snap a picture here is at sunset when sunlight is coming through the arc itself.

Address: Arc de Triomphe du Carrousel, 75001 Paris, France
Closest Subway Station: Palais Royal - Musée du Louvre
http://en.wikipedia.org/wiki/Place_du_Carrousel

6. Le Conciergerie

Located on the west of the île de la cité and right next door to Sainte Chapelle, Le Conciergerie is a former prison in Paris, open during the French Revolution, where the famous Marie Antoinette was imprisoned. The architecture here is absolutely stunning and definitely worth a tour and some photos. It is actually not that large of a place, so visitors will not spend too much time here; it is a perfect pit stop.

Address: 2 Boulevard du Palais, 75001 Paris, France
Closest Subway Station: Cité
http://fr.wikipedia.org/wiki/Palais_de_la_Cit%C3%A9

7. The Arc de Triomphe

The Arc de Triomphe is one of the most famous monuments in Paris. This famously imposing arc memorializes military victory and also marks the crossroads of twelve different streets. You can snap pictures from a variety of different locations, including the outer circle across from the Arc, the inner circle, and even from a good distance away in the middle of the Champs Elysees. You can also go up the arc and take some pictures from the top.

Address: Place Charles de Gaulle, 75008 Paris, France
Closest Subway Station: Kléber, George V
http://es.wikipedia.org/wiki/Arco_de_Triunfo_de_Par%C3%ADs

8. The Natural History Museum

Located on the left bank of the River Seine, the Natural History Museum provides some great opportunities for cool pictures. It was founded in 1793 during the French Revolution, but was actually established earlier in 1635. Its main attractions are the Hall of Evolution, the gallery of comparative anatomy (dinosaurs, giant birds, and insects), and the gallery of mineralogy, where you can take some insanely cool shots. Plus, the architecture is fabulous, with a wide, open interior, making for some great photo opportunities. Also note that the lights in the ceiling change colors, which creates nice tone changes in the atmosphere (and in the pictures).
Address: 6 Place Paul Painlevé, 75005 Paris, France
Closest Subway Station: Odéon
http://en.wikipedia.org/wiki/National_Museum_of_Natural_History_(France)

9. The Metro

The Metro station is a place to shoot some interesting pictures of daily neighborhood life. It is a great spot to take pictures of people going about their everyday lives and also of the many art nouveau station signs and things inside the extensive Metro network. If you are interested in an "attractive looking" metro station, the station near Notre Dame (called Cite) is interesting in terms of design and architecture. It is also filled with people!

Address: The Metro Cite, Paris, France
Closest Subway Station: Cite
http://en.wikipedia.org/wiki/Paris_M%C3%A9tro

10. Musee d'Orsay

Located on the left bank of the River Seine, this museum is actually an old train station! While the interior of the museum is great, the exterior can also be considered a work of art, and you can take some great photographs of the exterior at whatever time of day. Unfortunately, on the inside, there is a "no photograph" policy, but chances are you will be tempted to take some pictures of the interior architecture and scene -- just do not use flash when taking pictures of the paintings! You do not want to get caught taking pictures inside.
Address: 1 Rue de la Légion d'Honneur, 75007 Paris, France
Closest Subway Station: Solférino, Assemblée Nationale
https://commons.wikimedia.org/wiki/File:Mus%C3%A9e_d'Orsay_et_la_Seine.jpg

11. St. Paul-St. Louis Church

St. Paul-St.Louis is a 17th century church situated in the Marais district. This domed church was built by the Jesuits after a design inspired by the Gesu church in Rome. Like many churches, the exterior is not very ornamental, but the interior is definitely worth a visit and some snapshots. Some interesting things you can take pictures of inside include a grand organ built in 1867, a famous painting called *Christ on the Mount of Olives*, and the altar, which dates back to the 18th century and contains fragments of the Tomb of Napoleon in the Dome Des Invalides.

Address: 99 Rue Saint-Antoine, 75004 Paris, France

Closest Subway Station: Saint-Paul

http://commons.wikimedia.org/wiki/File:St-Paul-St-Louis-DSC_8039.jpg

12. Champs Elysees

This is without a doubt the most famous boulevard in Paris. At one end of the Champs Elysees is the Arc de Triomphe, and at the other end is basically the Louvre, so chances are you are very likely to walk through this boulevard. It is obviously a very touristy spot, but if you hang around after dark, you can find some interesting and beautiful scenes to point the camera at. If you are in Paris during Christmas time, this boulevard at night is decorated in beautiful lights -- it is quite the sight to see!

Address: Av. des Champs-Élysées, 75008 Paris, France
Closest Subway Station: Franklin D. Roosevelt
http://commons.wikimedia.org/wiki/File:Champs_Elysees_In_Paris_At_Night_II.jpg

13. Sacre Coeur

Sitting atop Montmartre, Sacre Coeur is one heck of a beautiful basilica. Sacre Coeur was built from contributions pledged by Parisian Catholics as an act of contrition after the Franco-Prussian War of 1870-71. Unfortunately, they do not allow photography inside, and because it is always packed with visitors and security guards, it is very difficult to snap shots (though not impossible). However, the exterior is just as impressive as the interior, not to mention the neighborhood around the area as well. The best time to take photos is when the sun is low on the horizon because the soft light makes the marble glow, casting colorful shadows from one dome to the next.

Address: 35 Rue du Chevalier de la Barre, 75018 Paris, France
Closest Subway Station: Château Rouge
https://en.wikipedia.org/wiki/File:Sacr%C3%A9-C%C5%93ur,_Paris_at_night.jpg

14. Les Invalides

Officially known as L'Hotel national de Invalides, this is a complex building in the 7th Arrondissement that contains museums and monuments all relating to the military history of France, as well as a hospital and a retirement home for war veterans, which was the building's original purpose. It is also the burial site for many of France's war heroes, most notably Napoleon Bonaparte! The interior is amazing and worth taking photos of. Plan to spend some time here snapping a lot of pictures of history and tombs!

Address: 129 Rue de Grenelle, 75007 Paris, France
Closest Subway Station: Varenne
http://commons.wikimedia.org/wiki/File:Les_Invalides_Paris.jpg

15. The Sorbonne

The Sorbonne is a public university in the Latin Quarter. Paris Sorbonne University is the main inheritor of the old Sorbonne, which dates back to the 13th century, making it one of the first universities in the world. The architecture here is absolutely stunning. The university is a great place to take photos during the day to capture not only the amazing architecture, but also on-campus student life.

Address: Sorbonne 1 rue Victor Cousin, 75230 Paris, France
Closest Subway Station: Cluny - La Sorbonne
http://en.wikipedia.org/wiki/Pantheon-Sorbonne_University

16. Luxembourg Gardens (Jardin du Luxembourg)

Created in 1612 by Marie de' Medici, the widow of King Henry IV of France, Luxembourg Gardens is located in the 6th Arrondissement. The Luxembourg Gardens, which covers about 23 hectares, is known for its lawns, tree-lined promenades, flowerbeds, model sailboats, and the picturesque Medici Fountain, which was built in 1620. The best season to shoot at the Luxembourg Gardens is in the spring, of course, but the other seasons are great for snapping some pictures as well! Take a walk through the park and relax in between photo sessions, or stop and have a picnic!
Address: 6th Arrondissement, 75006 Paris, France
Closest Subway Station: Rennes, Notre-Dame-des-Champs
https://en.wikipedia.org/wiki/File:Jardin_du_Luxembourg_en_%C3%A9t%C3%A9.jpg

17. Place de la Concorde

Place de la Concorde is one of the major public squares in Paris, and it is also the biggest. Located in the 8th Arrondissement, it is designed as an octagon between the Champs Elysees and the Tuileries Garden. The square is decorated with beautiful statues and fountains and is a super convenient place to shoot, since it sits between the Louvre and the Arc de Triomphe. Chances are you are going to visit at least one of these sights!
Address: 75008 Paris, France
Closest Subway Station: Concorde
https://en.wikipedia.org/wiki/Place_de_la_Concorde

18. Pont Alexandre III

This bridge is considered one of the most beautiful and ornate bridges in the city. It sits right in front of Les Invalides and crosses the River Seine, getting you from Les Invalides over to the Champs Elysees. Nighttime is a great time to shoot because the beautiful river and bridge are illuminated by lampposts, casting soft light perfect for amazing snapshots and portraits. During the day, shoot the beautiful bridge from a distance and you will get some awesome shots.

Address: Pont Alexandre III, Paris, France

Closest Subway Station: Invalides

https://en.wikipedia.org/wiki/Pont_Alexandre_III#/media/File:Pont-Alexandre-III-et-Invalides.jpg

19. Centre Pompidou

The Centre Pompidou houses a vast public library, the Museum of Modern Art, which is the largest museum for modern art in Europe, and IRCAM, a center for music and acoustic research. While this building is both a library and a museum, it is best known for its interesting architecture. All the buildings' systems are actually located on the outside and color-coded for easy reference! It is definitely a fascinating stop.

Address: Place Georges-Pompidou, 75004 Paris, France
Closest Subway Station: Rambuteau
https://en.wikipedia.org/wiki/File:Pompidou_center.jpg

20. Hotel de Ville

In the 4th Arrondissement, you will find Hotel de Ville, which is the city hall building for Paris. It has been the location of the municipality of Paris since 1357 and also serves other functions, like housing the local administration, the Mayor of Paris, and serving as a venue for large receptions. Because the building is so old, you can imagine how beautiful the architecture is. Any time of day is a great time to shoot, but later at night there are less people around. It is a short walk from Notre Dame, so you can get pictures of two places in one stroll.

Address: Place de l'Hôtel de ville, 75004 Paris, France

Closest Subway Station: Hôtel de Ville

https://de.wikipedia.org/wiki/H%C3%B4tel_de_Ville_(Paris)

21. Opera Garnier

Probably one of the most famous opera houses in the world, OperaGarnier is named after its architect, Charles Garnier, and is known for its opulence. It is a 2000-seat opera house that was built in 1861. The architecture is absolutely breathtaking. It costs about ten Euros to get in and is totally worth it. There is a ton of incredible ornate architecture inside that you can spend many hours photographing.

Address: 8 Rue Scribe, 75009 Paris, France
Closest Subway Station: Opéra, Chaussée d'Antin - La Fayette
http://en.wikipedia.org/wiki/Palais_Garnier

22. St. Etienne du Mont

St. Etienne du Mont is a lovely church located in the 5th Arrondissement near the Pantheon. The building is incredibly beautiful inside and out. The interior of the church is Gothic, which is an unusual style for a 16th-century church. It contains the shrine of St. Genevieve (the patroness saint of Paris) and the tombs of Blaise Pascal and Jean Racine. Go early in the morning so you have time to shoot inside and out.

Address: Place Sainte-Geneviève, 75005 Paris, France
Closest Subway Station: Place Monge
https://www.talkinfrench.com/best-secret-paris/

23. Versailles

Everyone knows about Versailles -- it was once the home of Louis XIV and others, but now it is just a wonderful palace with insanely awesome architecture and gardens. □It is roughly twelve miles outside of Paris, and a forty-minute ride by train. It is super easy to get to, and well worth a day of your time. The Palace of Versailles and grounds are precious settings for shooting photographs, and even better for shooting portraits.

Address: Place d'Armes, 78000 Versailles, France
Closest Subway Station: Versailles Rive Gauche

https://en.wikipedia.org/wiki/File:Vue_a%C3%A9rienne_du_domaine_de_Versailles_par_ToucanWings_-_Creative_Commons_By_Sa_3.0_-_073.jpg

24. Moulin Rouge

Another very famous site in Paris, Moulin Rouge is a sight to see. Once you get past the spinning windmill, the façade of the Moulin Rouge is not all that pretty. However, it is still iconic, and if you get creative, there are a number of other things to photograph in the Quartier Pigalle. This area is definitely a different side of Paris -- it may be worth it to snap some pictures of the not so "romantic" side of Paris.

Address: 82 Boulevard de Clichy, 75018 Paris, France
Closest Subway Station: Blanche
http://en.wikipedia.org/wiki/Moulin_Rouge

25. Les DeuxMagots

A famous café in the Saint-Germain-des-Pres area, Les DeuxMagots once had a reputation as the rendezvous spot of the literary and intellectual elite of the city. Its historical reputation is derived from the artists and young writers that frequented the café, like Simone de Beauvoir, Ernest Hemingway, and Pablo Picasso, to name a few. At night, when all the lights are lit and all the people are sitting at tables eating and chatting away, it makes for a beautiful shot of Parisian life at dinnertime.

Address: 6 Place Saint-Germain des Prés, 75006 Paris, France
Closest Subway Station: Mabillon
https://en.wikipedia.org/wiki/File:Lesdeuxmagots.jpg

26. Galeries Lafayette

Galeries Lafayette is an upscale mall found in the 9th Arrondissement. It has 10 floors, is very lavish, and has amazing architecture, which makes for some great pictures. The best time to take pictures here is during Christmas. At that time, the mall goes all out and suspends a beautiful giant Swarovski Christmas tree upside down in mid-air in the center of the mall -- how cool is that! Plus, you can do some shopping while you snap photos, too!

Address: 40 Boulevard Haussmann, 75009 Paris, France
Closest Subway Station: Chaussée d'Antin - La Fayette
http://commons.wikimedia.org/wiki/File:GaleriesLafayetteNuit.jpg

27. Rue St Severin and☐Rue de la Huchette

These two streets are very close to Notre Dame. They are filled with beautiful cafes, restaurants, bars, and shops. These streets are great places to take pictures of little café scenes, people watching, and everyday life in Paris.

Address: Rue de la Huchette, 75005 Paris, France

Closest Subway Station: Saint-Michel

http://commons.wikimedia.org/wiki/File:PC090068_Paris_V_Rue_des_pretres_de_Saint-Severin_reductwk.JPG

28. Galeries Vivienne

Located in the 2ᴺ Arrondissement, Galeries Vivienne is yet another shopping center, although very different from other shopping centers. It is much older and has a lot of character. Here, the beautiful architecture, delicate mosaics, and grand statues that are wonderfully preserved will have you snapping pictures for a while. Plus, you can visit the chic shops and eat at one of its restaurants while you are there. The glass roof also makes for great shooting during the day, adding natural light to your photographs.

Address: 6 Rue Vivienne, 75002 Paris, France
Closest Subway Station: Bourse
http://commons.wikimedia.org/wiki/File:P1040479_Paris_II_galerie_Vivienne_entr%C3%A9e_rw
k.JPG

29. The Church of Saint Severin

A Roman Catholic Church in the Latin Quarter of Paris is one of the oldest churches that remain standing on the Left Bank. This Gothic church is incredibly lovely and has some beautiful stained-glass windows, both old and modern, making an interesting contrast with the old architecture. Both the interior and exterior are worth photographing, and it is a perfect spot to stop on your way to Notre Dame.
Address: 1 Rue des Prêtres Saint-Séverin, 75005 Paris, France
Closest Subway Station: Cluny - La Sorbonne
https://en.wikipedia.org/wiki/File:Paris-St-Severin.JPG

30. Cemeteries

Does this sound eerie to you? Well, it's not too bad when there are fine stone carvings, beautiful backdrops, and iconic people lying there for their eternal rest. One such cemetery is Cimitiere du Pere Lachaise, where you can find the graves of Jim Morrison, Edith Piaf, Oscar Wilde, Moliere, Frederic Chopin, Marcel Proust, Honore de Balzac, and many other great artists and writers.

Address: 16 Rue du Repos, 75020 Paris, France
Closest Subway Station: Pere Lachaise

Source: https://commons.wikimedia.org/wiki/File:Cemetery_P%C3%A8re-Lachaise_-
_Division_27_-_vue_01.jpg

31. Shakespeare & Co bookstore

While you may not be thinking about visiting a bookstore while you are in Paris, Shakespeare & Co bookstore is definitely worth a visit. Today, it serves as a regular bookstore, a second-hand bookstore, and a reading library. The bookstore has been featured in a couple of movies as well. It is a fun little stop close to Notre Dame and is worth a couple of photographs.

Address: 37 Rue de la Bûcherie, 75005 Paris, France

Closest Subway Station: Cluny - La Sorbonne, Saint-Michel

https://en.wikipedia.org/wiki/File:Shakespeare_and_Company_store_in_Paris.jpg

32. Rue Mouffetard

Rue Mouffetard is a lovely little street full of shops and restaurants deep in the Latin Quarter, near Place Monge. Like other streets mentioned on this list, this lively street is great for taking pictures of a Parisian's everyday life and culture.
Address: Rue Mouffetard, 75005 Paris, France
Closest Subway Station: Censier - Daubenton, Place Monge
https://commons.wikimedia.org/wiki/File:Rue_Mouffetard,_Paris.jpg

33. Tour Montparnasse

The view at Tour Montparnasse is absolutely spectacular! It is a 210-meter office skyscraper, and the terrace on the top floor is open to the public, with an incredible view of the whole city. Fortunately, there are no time restrictions as to how long you can stay here, but it is recommended that you go early if you want a good spot to snap shots of the Parisian sunset.

Address: 33 Avenue du Maine, 75015 Paris, France
Closest Subway Station: Edgar Quinet
http://en.wikipedia.org/wiki/Tour_Montparnasse

34. Canal St-Martin

The serene Canal St-Martin stretches 4.5 kilometers from the Seine to Parc de la Villete in the 10ᵗʰ Arrondissement. It is probably one of the most quintessentially Parisian spots in the city where leisurely Parisians come on warm days to picnic, read books, and dip their feet in the cool water. Come on a sunny Sunday afternoon to take pictures of Parisians enjoying a leisurely afternoon in a beautiful area.

Address: Quai de Valmy, 75010 Paris, France
Closest Subway Station: Jacques Bonsergent
http://commons.wikimedia.org/wiki/File:P1040706_Paris_X_canal_Saint-Martin_rwk.jpg

35. Place des Vosges

One of the oldest squares in Paris, Place des Vosgesis located on the border of the 3rd and 4th Arrondissement in the Marais district. It is lined with elegant townhouses where people like Cardinal Richelieu and Victor Hugo once lived. The arched walkways that skirt the square are full of art galleries and cafes, too -- perfect for people-watching and taking pictures.

Address: Place des Vosges, 75004 Paris, France
Closest Subway Station: Chemin Vert
https://en.wikipedia.org/wiki/File:Paris_PlaceDesVosges_NordNordEst.JPG

36. Outdoor Café

Outdoor cafés are great places to shoot pictures -- you can truly capture the atmosphere of the city. At an outdoor café, you can take a seat, drink a cup of coffee, and snap pictures of what the real Paris is like, right from your table! Plus, there are a number of cafes to choose from, with people enjoying their time, cars zipping by, businesses opening and closing, all making for some awesome pictures of everyday Parisian life.

Address: 6 rue de Belzunce, 75010 Paris, France

Closest Subway Station: Gare du Nord

https://fr.wikipedia.org/wiki/Fichier:Caf%C3%A9_Delmas,_2_Place_de_la_Contrescarpe,_Paris_June_2008.jpg

37. Disneyland Paris

Of course Disneyland is going to be on the list! While not actually in Paris, despite its name, it is definitely worth the trek and time. Disneyland was designed to be a picturesque location, so you can imagine all the great photos you can take here. The most iconic photo to take at Disneyland Paris is of Le Chateau de la Belle au Bois Dormant. With some creativity, though, you can find a plethora of other great things to take pictures of.

Address: 77777 Marne-la-Vallée, France
Closest Subway Station: Marne La Vallee Chessy
https://en.wikipedia.org/wiki/File:Disneyland_Hotel,_Paris,_France,_2011.jpg

38. Cafes and shops

Like particular streets and outdoor cafes, cafes and shops are remarkable locations to take some spectacular pictures. Because life is always happening at these locations, you can shoot at any time of day and the pictures are bound to come out great.

Address: 52 rue de l'Hôtel de Ville 4e, Paris, France

Closest Subway Station: Saint-Paul

https://en.wikipedia.org/wiki/File:Caf%C3%A9_des_Phares,_Place_de_la_Bastille,_Paris.JPG

39. Jardin des Tuileries

These gardens by the Louvre form one of the world's longest architectural perspectives, running from the Louvre pyramids up to the Arc de Triomphe and beyond in the 1st Arrondissement. Statues are also scattered throughout the gardens; the best photographs are of people interacting with them. There are always people taking a stroll, hanging out, or having picnics in these gardens, too, so snapping at any time during the day is great.

Address: 113 Rue de Rivoli, 75001 Paris, France

Closest Subway Station: Concorde

http://en.wikipedia.org/wiki/File:Mus%C3%A9e_du_Louvre_-_from_Jardin_des_Tuileres,_Paris,_France_(26_April_2006).JPG

40. Bouquinistes

Along the River Seine, green metal stalls of bouquinistes display anything from books and magazines to postcards for sale. Go during the day and take some pictures of people in action buying products.

Address: 53 Quai des Grands Augustins, 75006 Paris, France
Closest Subway Station: Saint-Michel
http://en.wikipedia.org/wiki/Bouquinistes

II. Film Locations in Paris

As the city of romance, Paris has spent its fair share of time in the spotlight in many movies and TV shows through the years. Below is a list of Paris-based scenes, many of which you can actually visit on your trip to Paris. How many scenes will you be able to recognize when visiting these locations?

1. Quai de Montebello

Quai de Montebello has appeared in a number of movies. For example, in *An American in Paris* (1951), Gene Kelly serenades Leslie Caron here. Director Woody Allen pays homage to this scene, not just once, but twice! First, in *Everyone Says I Love You* (1996), and more recently in *Midnight in Paris* (2011).
Address: Quai de Montebello, 75005 Paris, France
Closest Subway Station: Cluny - La Sorbonne, Maubert - Mutualité
https://commons.wikimedia.org/wiki/File:Quai_de_Montebello,_Paris_13_April_2015.jpg

2. Rue Montagne Ste Genevieve

In *Midnight in Paris*, Rue Montagne Ste Genevieve is where Gil Pender (played by Owen Wilson) loves to hang out when the clock strikes twelve in the French capital, waiting for a taxi to take him back to the "Roaring Twenties."
Address: Rue de la Montagne Sainte Geneviève, 75005 Paris, France
Closest Subway Station: Cluny - Maubert - Mutualité
http://commons.wikimedia.org/wiki/File:Eglise_Saint_Etienne_du_Mont_(3749411570).jpg

3. Rue Chappe

Used in countless movies including *An American in Paris*, *Paris Blues* (1961), *Forget Paris* (2000), and *An Education* (2009), the Rue Chappe stairway seems to be Hollywood's favorite Montmartre location. The most popular is probably in *An American in Paris* when Leslie Caron and Gene Kelly make up in the final scene, at the top of the Rue Chappe, underneath the Sacre Coeur.

Address: Rue Chappe, 75018 Paris, France
Closest Subway Station: Abbesses
https://commons.wikimedia.org/wiki/File:Rue_Chappe_2,_Paris_September_15,_2012.jpg

4. Rue des Trois Frere

Also located in Montmarte, Rue des Trois Frere is where Amelie, from the movie *Amelie* (2001), lives (number 56 to be exact). It is also where she shops for groceries. In fact, the actual shopkeeper of the store liked the look given to his premises by the movie's Art Directors so much that he ended up keeping it, along with the MaisonCollignon sign over his shop.

Address: Rue des Trois Frere, 75018 Paris, France

Closest Subway Station: Abbesses

https://upload.wikimedia.org/wikipedia/commons/a/ae/20051018%C3%89picerie_d%27Am%C3%A9lie_Poulain_2.jpg

5. Rue Paul Albert

This street, a little further uphill from Rue des Trois Frere, is where Meg Ryan and Kevin Kline quarrel all the way down the street and decide to go their separate ways in *French Kiss* (1995).

Address: Rue Paul Albert, 75018 Paris, France
Closest Subway Station: Chateau Rouge
http://commons.wikimedia.org/wiki/File:P1040657_Paris_X_rue_Albert-Thomas_rwk.JPG

6. BirHakeim Bridge

Pont BirHakeim has been seen in many movies. Some notable mentions include *Last Tango* (1972), when Marlon Brando howls in pain in the opening scene, in Spielberg's *Munich* (2005), and, of course, in Christopher Nolan's *Inception* (2010). If you have seen *Inception*, you will instantly recognize the double-decker bridge where Leo DiCaprio and Ellen Page filmed one of the early scenes in which he teaches her about dream sharing.

Address: Quai de Grenelle, 75015 Paris, France
Closest Subway Station: Bir-Hakeim
http://en.wikipedia.org/wiki/Pont_de_Bir-Hakeim

7. Place de Marche Ste Catherine

You will see Place de Marche Ste Catherine is the global headquarters of the Treadstone organization where CIA agents devise a plan to kill the innocent in *The Bourne Identity* (2002).
Address: Place du Marché Sainte-Catherine, 75004 Paris, France
Closest Subway Station: Saint-Paul
https://commons.wikimedia.org/wiki/File:Le_March%C3%A9,_2_Place_du_March%C3%A9_Sainte-Catherine,_75004_Paris_2008.jpg

8. Nemours

Located just outside the beautiful Palais Royal, Le Nemours Cafe on Place Colette is where Angelina Jolie burns a letter and then flees from her enemy in the opening scene of the movie *The Tourist* (2010). It is also a brasserie where actors come often in the evening to dine, so you might get lucky and meet someone famous here!

Address: 2 Galerie Nemours, 75001 Paris, France

Closest Subway Station: Palais Royal/Musée du Louvre

https://commons.wikimedia.org/wiki/File:Chateau_de_Nemours_P1050505.jpg

9. Pont d'Arcole

Near the Hotel de Ville, Pont d'Arcole is seen in the final scene of *Something's Gotta Give* (2003). Just before the final credits, Jack Nicholson admits to himself that he has fallen in love after a nightly walk, and Diane Keaton happens to arrive just in time for a tear-jerking reunion.
Address: 4e Arrondissement, 75004 Paris, France
Closest Subway Station: Cite, Hotel de Ville
http://fr.wikipedia.org/wiki/Pont_d'Arcole

10. Rue Mouffetard

Movie fans will notice that Rue Mouffetard is where Meryl Streep finds the ingredients for her culinary experiences in *Julie and Julia* (2009). Rue Mouffetard is a beautiful street market, probably one of the most picturesque street markets in Paris!
Address: Rue Mouffetard, 75005 Paris, France
Closest Subway Station: Place Monge, Censier - Daubenton
http://commons.wikimedia.org/wiki/File:Rue_Mouffetard,_Paris.jp

11. Café des Deux Moulins

Amelie (2001) is a movie about contemporary Parisian life, set in Montmartre. In the movie, Amelie, who works as a shy waitress in Café des DeuxMoulins, decides to change the lives of those around her for the better. While you are here, take a seat and order a delicious dessert!
Address: 15 Rue Lepic, 75018 Paris, France
Closest Subway Station: Blanche
https://commons.wikimedia.org/wiki/File:Amelie,_Caf%C3%A8_des_2_moulins.jpg

12. Gare du Nord

You will recognize Gare du Nord from *The Bourne Identity* (2002), when Jason Bourne arrives in Paris with a duffel bag full of fake passports. Jason ditches the red bag in a locker at Europe's busiest railway station, which is also a Beaux-Arts architectural masterpiece.

Address: 18 Rue de Dunkerque, 75010 Paris, France

Closest Subway Station: Gare du Nord

https://commons.wikimedia.org/wiki/File:Gare_du_Nord_night_Paris_FRA_001.JPG

13. Carré Marigny

Romantic movie buffs will identify CarreMarigny as the bustling open-air market in the 8th Arrondissement where Cary Grant and Audrey Hepburn spy on James Coburn while creepy circus music plays in the background of the movie *Charade* (1963).

Address: CarréMarigny, 75008 Paris, France

Closest Subway Station: Champs-Élysées

https://fr.wikipedia.org/wiki/Th%C3%A9%C3%A2tre_Marigny

14. Promenade Plantée

In the movie *Before Sunset* (2004), the beautiful Promenade Plantee in the 12th Arrondissement is in the scene where Ethan Hawke and Julie Delpy take a stroll while talking about a special night from long ago.
Address: Quinze-Vingts, 75012 Paris, France
Closest Subway Station: Daumesnil
https://commons.wikimedia.org/wiki/File:Parigi_-_Promenade_plant%C3%A9e_IMG_8893.JPG

15. Da Stuzzi

In what is hailed as one of the best, if not the most mind-blowing, films of all time, *Inception* shot one of its key locations in Paris, in a café called the 'Debussy'. The Debussy is actually the Italian restaurant Da Stuzzi, located on the corner of rue Bouchut in the 7th Arrondissement. It is here where Cobb (Leonardo diCaprio) actually reveals to Ariadne (Ellen Page) that they are, in fact, inside a dream within a dream. The dream café explodes into pieces, but do not worry -- it was all just in a dream and Da Stuzzi is fine!

Address:6 rue Cesar Franck

Closest Subway Station:Sèvres - Lecourbe

Image source:
http://www.hotels-paris-rive-gauche.com/blog/2010/07/27/inception-paris-caprio-nolan-visit-sets/

16. Place Dauphine

Place Dauphine, a romantic spot for summer picnics, was shot in the final episodes of *Sex and the City* (2004) where Carrie and Aleksandr would stroll. It is a beautiful square to hang out and remember the show.
Address: 1st Arrondissement, 75001 Paris, France
Closest Subway Station: Cite
http://de.wikipedia.org/wiki/Place_Dauphine

17. The Louvre

The first and final scenes of *The Da Vinci Code* (2006) take place in the cavernous halls of the Louvre. You can pretend to be Tom Hanks and search for the "rose line," which is marked by small brass medallions and runs through the city.
Address: 75001 Paris, France
Closest Subway Station: Palais Royal
https://en.wikipedia.org/wiki/File:Louvre_2007_02_24_c.jpg

18. Pont Alexandre III

The last scene of *Midnight in Paris* (2011) is filmed in the impressive Pont Alexandre III. In this scene, Gil enjoys the enchanting views of Paris at night. It is also a popular spot where couples take their wedding and engagement photos in real life.
Address: Pont Alexandre III, Paris, France
Closest Subway Station: Invalides
https://commons.wikimedia.org/wiki/File:Pont_Alexandre_III,_Paris_8th_025.JPG

19. Chez Julien / Café Louis Philippe

This spot is a picture-perfect meeting location and looks like it is part of a small French village instead of a big city. In the show *Gossip Girl*, in season 4, Blair and Serena meet each morning in front of Chez Julien and Café Louis Philippe for a little rendezvous.
Address: 1 Rue du Pont Louis-Philippe, 75004 Paris, France
Closest Subway Station: Pont Marie
http://fr.wikipedia.org/wiki/Rue_de_l'H%C3%B4tel-de-Ville_(Paris)

20. La Tour d'Argent

Any Pixar fan should definitely come and visit La Tour d'Argent! In the movie *Ratatouille* (2007), it is the main inspiration for the fictional restaurant Gusteau's.
Address: 15 Quai de la Tournelle, 75005 Paris, France
Closest Subway Station: Jussieu
https://commons.wikimedia.org/wiki/File:La_Tour_dArgent_2012-10-27.jpg

21. Church of St. Etienne du Mont

This beautiful church is seen in *Midnight in Paris* (2011). Fans will recognize the scene when Gil is sitting on the steps outside of the church of St. Etienne du Mont and sees a car approaching at midnight.

Address: Place Sainte-Geneviève, 75005 Paris, France
Closest Subway Station: Cardinal Lemoine
http://en.wikipedia.org/wiki/Saint-%C3%89tienne-du-Mont

22. Rue Galande

In *Before Sunrise* (1995), Celine and Jesse are seen walking on the Left Bank on Rue Galande, passing the Studio Galande Cinema, which is a good place to catch an interactive showing of *The Rocky Horror Picture Show*.
Address: Rue Galande, 75005 Paris, France
Closest Subway Station: Cluny - La Sorbonne, Maubert - Mutualité
https://commons.wikimedia.org/wiki/File:P1240990_Paris_V_rue_Galande_n56_aux_trois_mailletz_rwk.jpg

23. Hotel Le Bristol

A luxurious 5-star Parisian hotel, Hotel Le Bristol is right smack in the middle of a high fashion shopping street, and where Gil and fiancée Inez in *Midnight in Paris* stay with her parents. Located in the 8th Arrondissement, many scenes were shot here, including the amusing scene where Gil tries to explain his dressed up appearance for his inspirational walks through Paris at night.

Address: 112 Rue du Faubourg-Saint-Honoré, Paris, France

Closest Subway Station: Champs-Élysées

https://commons.wikimedia.org/wiki/File:Mercedes_SLS_outside_Le_Bristol_Hotel,_Paris_August_2010.jpg

24. Le Grand Véfour

This historical restaurant opened in 1784 and is featured in another scene in *Midnight in Paris*. You will see Le Grand Vefour when Gil, Inez, and her family are having lunch. Located in the arcades of the lovely Palais Royal in the 1st Arrondissement, Le Grand Vefour exudes 18th century Parisian glamour.

Address: 17 Rue Du Beaujolais, 75001 Paris, France
Closest Subway Station: Palais Royal, Pyramides
https://fr.wikipedia.org/wiki/Fichier:P1050208_Paris_Ier_rue_de_Beaujolais_grand_Vefour_rwk. JPG

25. Musée Rodin, Hotel Biron

In *Midnight in Paris,* Gil and Inez visit the beautiful Rodin Museum in the 7th Arrondissement with Paul and Carol. While Paul walks through the gardens extolling his misinformed knowledge of Rodin, he is politely corrected by the museum guide. And Gil, who is taken by the museum guide, returns to ask her for help during his later adventures in Paris.

Address: 79 Rue de Varenne, 75007 Paris, France
Closest Subway Station: Varenne
http://en.wikipedia.org/wiki/Mus%C3%A9e_Rodin

26. Gertrude Stein's

GERTRUDE STEIN

1874 – 1946

ÉCRIVAIN AMÉRICAIN

Vécut ici avec son frère LÉO STEIN
puis avec ALICE B. TOKLAS
elle y reçut de nombreux
artistes et écrivains
de 1903 à 1938

This is where the second magical midnight takes place in *Midnight in Paris,* where Gil and Hemingway visit Gertrude Stein and her lover, Alice B Toklas, at the writer's real home. It is also here where Gil meets Pablo Picasso and his current, Mistress Adriana. The house is not open to the public, but a plaque above the door commemorates the writer's 33-year residence.

Address: 27 rue de Fleurus, 75006 Paris, France.
Closest Subway Station: Saint-Placide
https://en.wikipedia.org/wiki/Gertrude_Stein

27. Musée de l'Orangeri

Fans of *Midnight in Paris* will recognize Musee de l'Orangerie in the scene where the two couples visit the museum, admiring Monet's mesmerizing *Les Nympheas* paintings inspired by the gardens at Giverny.

Address: Jardin Tuileries, 75001 Paris, France

Closest Subway Station: Concorde

http://en.wikipedia.org/wiki/Mus%C3%A9e_de_l'Orangerie

28. Parc Jean XXIII

Parc Jean XXIII is seen in the scene in *Midnight in Paris* where Gil is amazed to find himself mentioned in Adriana's journal as it is read to him.

Address: 4e Arrondissement, 75004 Paris, France
Closest Subway Station: Cité

29. Maxim's, Rue Royale

In *Midnight in Paris,* Adriana and Gil are whisked further back to the Belle Epoque finery of Maxim's on Rue Royal, where scenes for the 1958 musical *Gigi* were filmed, and on to the Moulin Rouge, where painters Toulouse, Lautrec, Gauguin, and Degas hanker after the great age of the Renaissance.
Address: 3 Rue Royale, 75008 Paris, France
Closest Subway Station: Concorde
http://fr.wikipedia.org/wiki/Rue_Royale_(Paris)

30. Shakespeare and Company

Given his real life literary pursuits and his nighttime adventures with the likes of F. Scott Fitzgerald, Hemingway, and Gertrude Stein, just to name a few, it is no surprise that we see Gil leave the famous□Shakespeare and Company bookstore□just across the Seine from Notre Dame in *Midnight in Paris*.

Address: 37 Rue de la Bûcherie, 75005 Paris, France

Closest Subway Station: Saint-Michel, Cluny - La Sorbonne

http://en.wikipedia.org/wiki/Shakespeare_and_Company_(bookstore)

Conclusion
"Paris is always a good idea."

Audrey Hepburn uttered those unforgettable words in the classic 1954 movie *Sabrina*. To this day, it still rings true to hordes of travelers and tourists from all over the world. Paris, with its historic marvels and visually euphoric sights, has captivated the world many times over and continues to seduce and inspire people to come visit.

Now that you are on your very own Parisian holiday (or soon to travel), make the most of it by savoring the sights and preserving the memories with well-captured mementos. Hopefully, this handy little e-book can help you achieve just that.

Should you need more details about Paris, do not hesitate to take a look at my website www.talkinfrench.com. There are plenty more lists, insightful tidbits of information, as well as truckloads of details about France. You can also subscribe to my mailing list for your weekly dose of everything French: language topics, travel, culture, and many other things that I am sure you will love.

Merci beaucoup. I wish you a lovely time in Paris.

31624787R00098

Made in the USA
Middletown, DE
06 May 2016